D1084816

THE
BATTLE OF
THE ALMA

GREAT BATTLES OF HISTORY

Hanson W. Baldwin, GENERAL EDITOR

Also by Peter Gibbs

A FLAG FOR THE MATABELE

CRIMEAN BLUNDER

THE
BATTLE OF
THE ALMA

PETER GIBBS

63P2I7x

947.07 G446

DK
215.1
.G5

J. B. LIPPINCOTT COMPANY
Philadelphia & New York

Copyright © 1963 by Peter Gibbs
First Edition
Printed in the United States of America
Library of Congress Catalog Card Number: 63–8888

Maps by Robert and John Hallock

FOREWORD

History, I maintain, should be taught backwards. First we should learn all we can of the events of our own time and then work back into the past along the chain of causation. Then we would find that the events of history are really not so inexplicable and far away in time after all.

I can remember as a small boy seeing some of the surviving Crimean veterans taking their senile ease among the Chelsea Pensioners—wrinkled but hale old men in their eighties, white-haired and ruddy-faced, as soldierly as ever in their scarlet pensioners' uniforms. A few of these men were still alive when the First World War ended. So, because in my lifetime I have seen men who fought in the Crimea, and during that same lifetime John Glenn has orbited the earth, there is for me a contemporaneous link between Cape Canaveral in 1962 and the Alma River in 1854. To take this fancy a little farther, since the men of the Crimea whom I saw fought beside the veterans of Wellington's armies, the tangible link runs back to Waterloo, even Corunna, and so on into history.

Admittedly, none of the modern refinements of fighting had been introduced at the time of the Crimean War. Soldiers fought standing shoulder to shoulder in ranks, exchanging musket fire with the enemy at point-blank range. The weapons were so inaccurate that casualties were light by our standards. But, primitive as their military science seems to us today, they were our contemporaries only once or twice removed. So I maintain that properly to understand events like the Crimean War we have to look at them as being one with the current scene.

Thus the battles of the Crimean War were fought, not a hundred years ago, but yesterday—and yesterday, of course, is followed by today.

Bulawayo,   PETER GIBBS
Southern Rhodesia
April, 1962

AUTHOR'S NOTE

The following places referred to in the text have since been renamed: Constantinople is Istanbul; St. Petersburg is Leningrad; Varna is Stalin (unless its name has been altered again); and Palestine is, of course, Israel.

P. G.

CONTENTS

LIST OF MAPS
AND DIAGRAMS

THE
BATTLE OF
THE ALMA

"I suppose one day the British soldier will be treated with humanity by his officers and his country. I hope so. He is, for all his faults, a noble creature."

FIELD MARSHAL LORD RAGLAN

1

TURKEY AND RUSSIA

Scattered about the world are scores of little towns and villages, rivers and streams, hills and mountain passes, whose names are eternally familiar merely because they recall a scene of battle. Thermopylae, Agincourt, Bannockburn, Blenheim, Bunker Hill, Waterloo, Bull Run, El Alamein—all are names that would have remained in comfortable obscurity, unmarked on any but the most parochial maps, had they not once been battlefields.

The Alma River is another of these names. Had it not been that, in 1854, this little river happened to become the line on which the armies of Britain and France encountered those of Russia, no one—except the handful of people who have lived along the Alma or crossed it in their journeyings—would ever have heard of it.

Nevertheless, the Crimea itself was probably destined to achieve some sort of special notoriety, if only because of its peculiar geographical characteristics. A peninsula protruding conspicuously into the otherwise unbroken coastline of the Black Sea, it is almost completely detached from the Russian mainland. But for the slender little Perekop isthmus—in some parts not more than three or four miles wide—by which it is connected to the continental mass, the Crimea would have been an island, and the waters that would have separated it from the mainland might well have insulated it from much of the turbulence that over the centuries has beset southeastern Europe and often spilled over onto Crimean soil.

The area of the Crimea is no more than 10,000 square miles —about the size of Maryland, without the Chesapeake Bay. Most of the country is steppe, that treeless plain of which so much of Russia consists. From the Perekop isthmus, the Crimean steppe rises gently towards the south, so that in winter this stretch of open country lies exposed to the savage, icy blasts that sweep perennially southward across the equally treeless and featureless expanses of the Ukraine. In early spring, when the winds begin to lose their ferocity and the snow begins to melt, the thick, tufted grass that carpets the steppe bursts forth in a profusion of lilies and aloes, agapanthus and wild hyacinth, and an herb that has a hint of lavender in its scent. But by the end of the summer the wild flowers have disappeared; the grass, parched by the sun, is bleached almost white; and whatever bare earth there is, is dust. Even the few lakes, which sparkle in the sunshine during the early summer, shrink towards their centers, leaving their gently shelving rims caked white by salt. Away from these saline lakes, whose waters are undrinkable, the only water is that raised from artesian wells, many of which were first sunk centuries ago. In September 1854, when the British and French armies came to the Crimea, there were villages dotted here and there, round which for thousands of years the peasants had grazed their goats and sheep and grown their sparse crops of wheat, but there was little else, and the northern steppe seemed empty and forsaken.

A range of mountains, the Yaila Dagh, runs along the south-

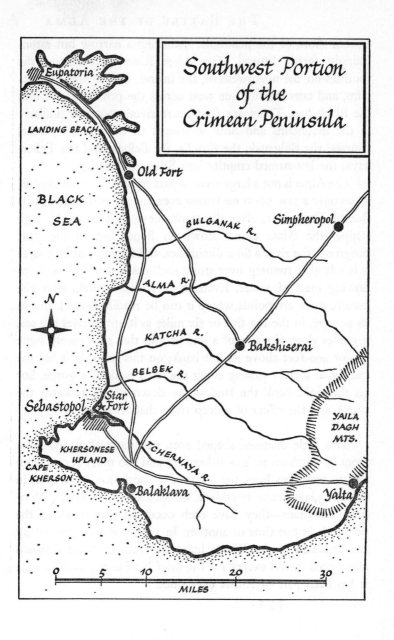

Southwest Portion of the Crimean Peninsula

Eupatoria

LANDING BEACH

Old Fort

BLACK SEA

BULGANAK R.

Simpheropol

ALMA R.

KATCHA R.

Bakshiserai

BELBEK R.

Star Fort

Sebastopol

KHERSONESE UPLAND

CAPE KHERSON

TCHERNAYA R.

YAILA DAGH MTS.

Balaklava

Yalta

N

0   5   10   20   30

MILES

eastern shore of the peninsula, sheltering a narrow but astonishingly fertile littoral. The Alma River rises among the foothills on the northwestern, the inland, face of these mountains, and cuts its way due west across the peninsula, out into the Black Sea. There are four more rivers that rise similarly in the mountains and flow westward to the sea on parallel courses: the Bulganak, the Katcha, the Belbek, and the Tchernaya; the last-named empties into Sebastopol harbor.

The Alma is not a large river. Apart from being unnavigable, it has only a few pools on which even the smallest boat can be floated. Each year, after the snows have melted on the high steppe, the Alma comes down in flood, but as the year progresses the river's flow diminishes, and for most of its course it is a freshet running over stony shallows rather than a deep-flowing mass of water. Even at its widest stretch, near the mouth, there are points where it can be readily forded. But in its passage, in the last five or six miles as it approaches the sea, it moves along the side of a line of hills that rise steeply some 300 or 400 feet above its left bank; on this left side it has the quality of a river passing along the deep bank of a gorge, but on the right bank the land slopes down gently towards the water, and the effect of a deep river channel is lost.

This little diamond-shaped area, not more than 100 miles from its northern to its southern tip and 200 miles across from east to west, has been the home of a succession of peoples in the last 3,000 years: Scythians, Greeks, Goths, Khazars, Mongols, Venetians—they have each occupied part or all of the peninsula at one time or another. In 1475 it was conquered by the Ottoman Turks. Three hundred years later the Russians conquered it, and except for the brief Nazi occupation in 1942 it has been part of Russia ever since.

The struggle between Russia and Turkey, which started in the sixteenth century, resulted from a variety of causes. It was basically a struggle for power, although the pretense was made that it was a struggle for rights. Like any conflict between two nations, it was confused by the pressures applied by other nations with a stake in the outcome. Of the two main contenders, Russia and Turkey, one was in the early stages of its ascent to world power, the other very nearly in the final stages of its decline from a position, if not of actual world power, at least of decisive authority in its own part of the world. Russian influence had really only begun to make itself felt during the reign of Catherine II, in the latter part of the eighteenth century; but thenceforth Russia was to move steadily toward its apogee of power in the twentieth century. The Ottoman Empire, on the other hand, had been born 600 years before, in the thirteenth century, and in the course of time its influence had spread far afield. Although the seeds of its decline germinated within itself, its real dissolution was set in motion by the ambitions of the Empress Catherine of Russia and was furthered by the Tsars who succeeded her. Nicholas I, in 1852, called Turkey "the sick man of Europe," the implication being that the Ottoman Empire was about to die. (It died finally at the end of the First World War.)

At the end of the eighteenth century, this conflict between Russia and Turkey was the principal element in what was popularly known in western Europe as "the Eastern Question." The core of the question concerned control of the trade routes to the Indies. Neither the Suez Canal nor the Middle Eastern sources of oil had come along to shift the center of gravity in that part of the world from the Ottoman Empire to the Arab countries. Going overland to the Indies still meant following caravan routes over the mountains of Asia Minor or Syria and dropping down to the East by way of the valley of the Euphrates. So the Turkish Empire was an essential link between western Europe and the East, and only by favoring Turkey —sometimes against their better judgment—could the nations of western Europe frustrate Russia's ambitions to cut them off from the East altogether.

The eastern tip of the Crimean peninsula controls the narrow little outlet into the Black Sea from the almost land-locked Sea of Azov, which in its turn is the outlet of that great Russian waterway, the River Don. The conflict between Russia and Turkey had come to be centered round yet another outlet: the Bosporus and the Dardanelles, which link the Black Sea and the Mediterranean. And since whoever holds the Crimea also controls the mouth of the Don, the Crimea has a strategic importance out of all proportion to the value of the land itself. For it has never had any special economic value, and only the narrow riviera along its southeastern coast endows it with any intrinsic attraction. It does, however, possess a magnificent natural harbor, on which the Russians built their naval base at Sebastopol.

The struggle between Russia and Turkey for control of the Black Sea was complicated by religious factors, for, in the middle of the nineteenth century, although the Turks as a people were Mohammedans, at least 15,000,000 Orthodox Christians were among the heterogeneous population that comprised the Turkish Empire. Consequently the Tsar of Russia, as the acknowledged champion of these people's church, exercised an influence within the Turkish Empire that was disturbing to the European powers. There was in fact a fifth column in Turkey that would undoubtedly give aid to any Russian military attack.

In 1850, Louis Napoleon, the self-created Emperor of

The "Eastern Question"

France, further complicated the situation. He was beset by two ambitions: to emulate the achievements of his illustrious uncle and to impress himself upon Tsar Nicholas as an imperial figure of some consequence. Knowing that it would annoy Nicholas, he demanded of the Turks that they give to the Roman Catholics in Palestine—which was then part of the Turkish Empire —full rights of access to the Holy Places, equal to those that had for many years been given, at Russia's insistence, to the members of the Orthodox Church. A petty quarrel between Roman Catholic and Greek monks in Bethlehem, over possession of keys to the Church of the Holy Sepulchre, was used to fan the dispute, which Louis Napoleon raised to the diplomatic level by instructing the French ambassador in Constantinople to demand from the Turkish government concessions that he was sure would be strongly contested by the Russians. The argument went on for three years, and inevitably Britain, afraid of undue Russian influence in Turkey, was drawn into it.

The crisis came in April 1853, when the Tsar sent, as his special envoy to Constantinople, one Prince Menshikov—whom we shall meet again later as the commander of the Russian army at the Battle of the Alma. Prince Menshikov was an imperious bully whose attitude to the Turks was hardened by bitterness over his emasculation by a shot from a Turkish gun. The Tsar ordered him to insist on two things: maintenance of exclusive privileges for orthodox Christians in the Holy Places, and the granting to Russia of a protectorate over Christians throughout the whole of the Turkish Empire. If the Turks refused these demands, he was to present them with an ultimatum.

The British ambassador in Constantinople, Viscount Stratford de Redcliffe, persuaded the Turks to give way to the

Russians in the matter of privileges in the Holy Places, advising them at the same time to stand firm on their refusal to give Russia the protectorate powers she was demanding.

Menshikov rejected outright the Turks' refusal to grant Russia her protectorate. He gave them three days to change their minds, and when, at de Redcliffe's prompting, they declined to do so, he returned to the Tsar at St. Petersburg. Nicholas ordered the advance of two army corps that had been waiting for some months on the Russian side of the Prut River for just such an eventuality.

The Prut River is a tributary of the Danube, which it joins less than seventy miles from the Black Sea coast. It forms the southwestern boundary of Russia, and the country on its right bank, which is Romania today, consisted in the middle of the last century of a number of principalities over which the Sultan of Turkey exercised a nominal suzerainty. Any Russian incursion into these principalities, although not an invasion of Turkey itself, could be regarded as indicative of the Tsar's ultimate intentions. The western powers hurriedly convened at Vienna, but the deadlock between Russia and Turkey persisted, and on October 23, 1853, Turkey declared that unless Russia withdrew her troops across the Prut a state of war would exist. The Russian armies remained where they were, and the two countries were formally at war.

The Russian and Turkish armies were still some hundreds of miles apart, and with winter approaching, the chances of immediate hostilities were slight. But little more than a month later, on November 30, the Russian Black Sea fleet sailed from Sebastopol to attack a squadron of the Turkish fleet as it lay at anchor in Sinop harbor, on the southern Black Sea shore. The Russian ships were so heavily armed that they were able to bombard and destroy the whole Turkish squadron and most of

[9]

the town of Sinop without coming within range of Turkish guns. The action was nothing short of a massacre, and three-fourths of the 4,000 Turkish sailors were killed. Every Turkish ship was destroyed, except for a small steamer that managed to slip away to Constantinople with the news and a frigate that the Russians captured.

Although the Russian attack was a legitimate act of war, the world received the news of the holocaust at Sinop with horror, and from that day on, in England and France, there rose an irresistible tide of hatred for Russia. Sebastopol, whence the Russian fleet had set out, became the special object of execration in Britain, until the desire for its destruction became almost a national aberration. Public hysteria grew in intensity as the months went by, until, in March 1854, the British and French governments were swept helplessly into the flood. Both declared war on Russia without even offering a rational motive for their action. During the next few weeks, 25,000 British and 30,000 French troops converged on Constantinople.

2

THE BELLIGERENTS

U<small>P TO THE BEGINNING</small> of the nineteenth century Britain had, for generations, almost continuously been involved in war. But in the forty years since 1815, when the Napoleonic menace had finally been disposed of, Britain had enjoyed uninterrupted peace, and with it social revolution that led to an expansion of wealth on a scale unpredecented in history.

This was not a climate to promote a spirit of militarism. In those days a country that was economically strong and whose people were manifestly prosperous and contented had no interest in pursuing military adventures. Britain was expanding her empire and her markets by overseas colonization, a pursuit that required a minimum of military force on land, since the only people she had to fight were natives with primitive weapons. During the years 1815–55, the belief grew in Britain that as long as she maintained her strength at sea her imperial status was virtually unassailable. The need for an army, other than to protect the outposts of her empire from local dangers —which were inconsiderable by European military standards— was discounted by almost everyone.

The result was that the British army came to be almost

entirely neglected. The expense of providing an army to look after their ever-expanding overseas interests was something the British people were prepared to accept. But any suggestion that the British army needed to be brought up to date would imply that Britain was likely to find herself at war, not with Kaffir tribes or Afghan hillmen, but with a civilized western power; and that, in the light of contemporary thinking, was absurd. After the collapse of Napoleon, there seemed no reason why Britain should ever again have to fight anyone on the continent of Europe.

Britain's greatest soldier, the Duke of Wellington, did not agree with, but was obliged to accept, this line of thinking. He feared that any attempt on his part to persuade the British people that money was needed for their army might instead start them questioning whether even the present cost of the army was justified. When the Duke died in 1852, in his eighty-third year, no one was left who personified the departed days of British military glory, and concern for the army receded farther than ever into the background.

There were, in the army itself, few officers, except those serving in India and the colonies or those old enough (sixty or over) to have fought in the Napoleonic wars, who had any experience of active service. Most of the younger officers entered the army, not because of interest in soldiering as a career, but because the army was a fashionable place for young aristocrats with no aptitude for any other profession but with the wealth needed to buy a commission.

In the ranks, the old soldiers who enlisted for life—a custom that continued until 1847—were dying off, and the average age of the troops was beginning to drop. The younger men not only had no experience of fighting but were not even trained for war. In Britain, life in the army simply meant barrack-square drill, rehearsed and repeated until every man became virtually an automaton and until the drill movements were made with a unison and a mechanical perfection that even the smartest units of today can hardly hope to equal. In theory, all drill was based on tactical movements for deploying troops in action—battles were still fought by soldiers in close formation—and ceremonial parades were merely adaptations of these movements. But in the British army, more than in any other army at the time, ceremony had become an end in itself, and the need to relate drill to actual tactical movements was apt to be entirely ignored. Officers spent their whole military careers moving their soldiers backward and forward across the parade ground, with never a thought of taking their companies into the fields and woods to simulate war maneuvers.

When the soldiers were not drilling, they were cleaning and refurbishing the elaborate, gaudy uniforms that had been developed for no other reason than ceremonial affectation. Commanding officers outdid one another in designing exotic headdresses and elaborate trappings for their regiments, making it more and more difficult for the men to keep their uniforms spotless, as they were required to do. In the massive stone barracks, which had been built during the Napoleonic wars, the soldiers lived virtually on top of one another, with hardly room to move. Living conditions in the barracks, particularly before the Crimean War and before the first seeds of reform had been sown in the British army, were appalling, and impeccable cleanliness and smartness was maintained only by terrible, almost inhuman, disciplinary measures.

Quite understandably, the only men who could be recruited into the army were those unwanted elsewhere. If a man was not an outcast from society before he enlisted as a soldier, he became one immediately after. And the discipline to which he was subjected did nothing to re-establish his self-respect. He had but to parade in a dirty uniform, or to show the slightest unsteadiness in his drill, and he was flogged with a cat-o'-nine-tails—not perhaps as severely as if he had mutinied or deserted, but flogged nevertheless. In this new era of liberalism, when slavery had been abolished throughout the Empire and even the prisons in Britain had been improved, the private soldier was treated with a callousness and brutality that would have brought howls of protest from the public in another context. He was paid a shilling a day, sixpence of which was deducted for rations. Nor was the balance sacrosanct. There were many other stoppages from his pay—fines, uniform replacements, and a host of regimental impositions. What little money he did get, he spent on drink, because society offered him nothing else. He had no clothes of his own, so he lived in uniform year in and year out, and most of his time when sober was spent in repairing the ravages of his drunken brawls and his squalid assignations.

Yet from this unpromising material a British army was to go to the Crimea that was to amaze the world by its fortitude and endurance. The story of the part played by the British in the Crimean War—their blunderings, their ineptitude—is not one of the more shining pages in that nation's history. The blame must not be laid on the soldiers but on those who directed the war—those who sent the soldiers to the Crimea in the first place and those who commanded them when they were there. It was the rank and file—the drunken, immoral outcasts from society—who saved the leaders from themselves. Repeatedly—on the banks of the Alma, at Balaklava, on the heights of Inkerman, and in the assault on Sebastopol itself—the soldiers retrieved the day after the generals had done everything possible to cast it away.

[14]

It is easy enough, when we consider the army that Britain sent to the Crimea, to attribute the soldiers' behavior in battle to the effect of appallingly harsh discipline (and perhaps to the insensitiveness of men whose lives had been spent in drink and debauchery). Men like these, we might say, would obey orders without question, would stand and fight to the end, if only because of their overmastering fear of punishment. That, of course, was the intention of those in authority who resisted any alleviation of the system. Yet when we examine more closely how these men behaved at the Battle of the Alma, we may well be inclined to modify our judgment of the quality of the British troops in the mid-nineteenth century.

Compared with the tranquillity and prosperity that had settled over England, the French scene during the first half of the nineteenth century was turbulent enough. It could hardly have been otherwise in the backwash of one of the most radical revolutions in history. By 1848, the Bourbon regime, after its brief restoration, had come to its inevitable end and the Second Empire, with Louis Napoleon as emperor, had been born.

Unlike the British army, whose structure had remained virtually static for fifty years, the French army had made considerable advances. After Waterloo, early in the restoration period, conscription—which had originally been introduced by Napoleon I—was for a time suspended. It was reintroduced in the 1830's, however, with the conquest and colonization of Algeria. Conscription assured that the new French army was made up of a representative selection of French citizens and would never become a mere receptacle for undesirables, like the British army of the same period.

The adventures of the French in Algeria were parallel to those of Britain in her quest for empire, with one important difference. Algeria was on the doorstep of metropolitan France, a short sea journey away, not at the other end of the world. Troops who embarked at Marseilles or Toulon were in action within a few days, and unlike the British soldiers overseas they could not be kept from the public notice. As a result, during the twenty years preceding the Crimean War, the need for an efficient army had been kept constantly before the French public. Although commissions could still be bought while the Bourbons were on the throne, democratization of the army was a continuing heritage of the Revolution, and promotion from the ranks, on the basis of merit, became a regular practice.

Although the fighting in Algeria may not have been on the scale of the great European wars of the past (as enemies, the Algerian tribes were more of the caliber of the Afghan hillmen who were the main adversaries of the British army), it took place so close to home that the French people could not help but appreciate its severity and the demands it made on the army. They realized, too, that the only way to wage war successfully is with an efficient and modern army. Consequently, by the 1840's France was a comparatively advanced military power. Most of her soldiers had already seen active service, and they were self-reliant and experienced enough so as not to require harsh discipline. Her officers were, for the most part, ambitious men, wholly dedicated to their profession; her generals were comparatively young and had discarded the theories and practices of the Napoleonic wars—by which all military thought in Britain was still regulated.

Louis Napoleon's *coup d'état* in 1848 brought new, less able, men into the officer corps of the French army. This new hierarchy consisted for the most part of men whom Napoleon could manipulate—men who were qualified less by their ability than by their pliability. St. Arnaud, Canrobert, Forey, Pélissier were names that were to become familiar in the Crimean War. St. Arnaud commanded the French army, and Canrobert and Forey each headed a division at the Battle of the Alma. When St. Arnaud died a few days after the battle, Canrobert succeeded him in command and was later replaced by Pélissier, who was the only one of these new generals to prove himself of any worth.

Russia, the third of the great powers involved in the Crimean War, was, by the middle of the nineteenth century, under a harsher tyranny than she had ever before known. Rebellion, fomented by the younger nobility who had learned of the social upheavals in western Europe, was already simmering. The first warning of a revolution—which was not to take place for nearly a hundred years—came on December 14, 1825, the day Nicholas I succeeded to the tsardom. One regiment mutinied in St. Petersburg and another marched on Kiev, but Nicholas acted quickly and firmly to put down the insurrection. The "Decembrists," the insurgents against whom the Tsar took terrible retribution, were the first martyrs of the Russian Revolution.

So, from the very outset of his reign, Nicholas was driven to adopt a policy of repression, and for this purpose he maintained a standing army three-quarters of a million strong—a tremendous force for any nineteenth-century nation to support. Nicholas' regime grew progressively harsher and more repressive, until in the 1840's and 1850's his people were living in a state of almost unmitigated servitude. Regimentation was everywhere, and nearly everyone was subjected to inhuman degradation. Brutal whipping for the most trivial offenses was so common that the Tsar was referred to by his own people as Nicholas the Flogger.

Conditions in the Russian army were such that those in the British army were benevolent by comparison. A relentlessly regimented and disciplined conscript force to which every man in Russia was bound to contribute his service, its strength lay solely in its numbers. Nicholas used it repeatedly to suppress internal uprisings, and he expected it to be just as effective in time of war.

3

DEVIOUS JOURNEY

TURKEY DECLARED war against Russia in July 1853, but the Russians, after crossing the Prut, made no significant advance southward until the following spring. Then they moved along the right bank of the Danube, upstream toward a Turkish fortress at Silistria, whence the road to Constantinople struck southward across the Bulgarian plain. On more than one occasion in the past, the Turks had held up a Russian invasion at Silistria. Now once again, for thirty-four hectic days in May and June 1854, the Russians besieged Silistria and the Turks withstood them in almost continuous battle. What the fighting lacked in science it made up for in ferocity, and by the time the siege was lifted the Russians had suffered 12,000 casualties.

Abdul-Mejid I, the Sultan of Turkey, and his father, Mahmoud II, had done much to westernize the Turkish army during the preceding thirty years. They introduced French and Prussian instructors, and at the time of the siege there was even a Prussian engineer in Silistria who was responsible for the fortifications. Also present unofficially on the Turkish side in Silistria were two young English officers who had made their way across Bulgaria and taken a significant part in directing the town's defense, although holding no authority whatsoever. By all accounts their part in rallying the defenders was a decisive factor in the outcome of the siege, whose lifting in the middle of June meant that the Russian advance on Constantinople was effectively halted.

A little later, a second Russian army, some 60,000 strong—commanded by a certain Prince Gorchakov (later to fight at the Alma)—assembled at Guirgevo, fifty miles upstream from Silistria, but retreated towards Bucharest as soon as it was attacked by a Turkish force, the Turks again being aided and abetted by a handful of British officers. The Russian withdrawal entirely removed the threat to Constantinople and to the independence of Turkey and made invalid Britain's and France's reasons for declaring war on Russia. The situation no longer seemed explosive, nor did there appear to be any differences between the great powers that could not be resolved by peaceful negotiation.

But by now both Britain and France had sent their armies to the Levant, and neither government felt itself disposed to deny its soldiers what was believed to be a providential chance to win military honors. In France, the direction of national policy was wholly in the hands of the Emperor, whose conceit was flattered and self-doubts appeased by the realization that he was in active alliance with a queen, and that even if the Tsar of Russia disdained to recognize him, Victoria of England formally acknowledged him as her royal equal. If Britain wished to continue the war, he was happy enough to go along. In any event, military adventure seemed a necessity to him, for he knew he could never consolidate his position with his own people until he had emulated at least some of his uncle's martial triumphs.

Britain's determination to continue the war was purely

emotional, and her government's decision merely reflected public belligerency. Britain had enjoyed peace for so long that none of her people had any idea what war implied. When anyone did mention the battles of half a century ago he talked only of victories, so that to the average Englishman war and victory were synonymous.

Twenty-five thousand soldiers set sail for the Levant, in February and March 1854, in an orgy of extravagant public enthusiasm. Whenever the regiments paraded and marched to their ports of embarkation, crowds cheered them wildly and everybody remarked on the faultlessness of their bearing and their obvious destination for victory. Overnight, the British soldier changed in the eye of the public from outcast to hero. That he was being sent to fight in a war that would be waged thousands of miles from home made it all the easier to show him this appreciation—although none of the people who were so ready to applaud him showed any concern over the dreadful conditions under which he served.

When the troops sailed from England, no one told them where they were going—not for any reasons of security but because their final destination had not yet been decided. Russian troops were known to be advancing on Constantinople southward through Bulgaria, and in an effort to create a second front the allies had already sent a joint military and naval expedition to the Baltic Sea, which was to prove quite abortive. But although it was known that the Russians would be coming through the principalities along the Danube, there was no agreement on where the enemy should be met in battle. Some believed the allies should throw a ring around Constantinople and wait for the Russians to come—and an English colonel of engineers, whose ideas were influenced by the retreat to

Corunna, in which he had taken part forty-six years before, had worked out a system of defensive positions.

The British transports first stopped at Malta. The French, who were starting from Mediterranean ports anyway, sailed through the Dardanelles and landed, at the end of March, at Gallipoli town, in European Turkey. Shortly afterwards, the British followed. But the town was overcrowded and shockingly dirty, and outside of the town there was no fresh water, so the British troops were compelled to move on through the Sea of Marmara to the Turkish garrison town of Scutari, at the entrance to the Bosporus itself, on the Asia Minor shore. The town was no more attractive than Gallipoli, but the countryside was fresher and more habitable. The British commander in chief, Lord Raglan, set up headquarters in Scutari, and here some of the British troops moved into those infamous barrack buildings where Florence Nightingale was only a few months later to create the immortal legend of the Lady with the Lamp.

While the British and French armies were encamping in Turkey, the Turks were themselves still fighting desperately to hold off the Russians at Silistria.

At last, nearly two months after war had been declared, the British and French commanders in chief recognized the need for a conference. Lord Raglan and Marshal St. Arnaud had first been introduced some weeks earlier in Paris, in a meeting of British and French military leaders under the chairmanship of Louis Napoleon. But at the meeting no attempt had been made to discuss strategy.

Lord Raglan, who was sixty-six, had spent almost all his military life as aide-de-camp and military secretary to the Duke of Wellington. Although he had seen enough fighting forty years earlier in the Peninsula and Waterloo campaigns—he had lost an arm in the latter—he had never previously held an independent command of any sort. All his fighting experience had been against Napoleon's armies, and throughout the Crimean War he was to be unable to discard completely the habit of referring to the enemy as the French, even when speaking in French, to French officers.

Raglan's experience, too, was primarily administrative, as all matters of strategy had been decided by the Duke, who had never even asked his officers' opinions—indeed, whenever the officers had a decision to make, they asked themselves what the Duke would do in the circumstances. After Wellington retired, there had been no need to think about strategy.

Raglan's age, seniority, and aristocratic position provided him with the authority and bearing of a commander. As the youngest son of the Duke of Beaufort, he had from birth enjoyed the title Lord FitzRoy Somerset. Granted a peerage after forty-nine years' service in the army, he became the first Lord Raglan. From the age of twenty, when he had first been made the Duke's aide-de-camp (his father had bought his commission for him while he was still at school), he had breathed the atmosphere of high military rank and the sense of assurance that went with it.

Marshal St. Arnaud was a soldier in quite a different mold. Only fifty-three, he had had an undistinguished career. For some discreditable reason, he had once resigned his commission and left the army. After some years he was recommissioned but on a later occasion he was reduced in rank following a lapse in discipline. He was one of the officers whom Louis Napoleon had arbitrarily lifted from obscurity at the time of the *coup d'état;* until then he had never consorted with men in positions of high command, and his limited experience of affairs left him with a naïve approach to responsibility. At the meeting in Paris, he had deliberately avoided discussing his plans. His purpose became apparent soon after he and Raglan arrived in Turkey. He informed Raglan, quite mendaciously, that the Turks—who were 200 miles away holding back the Russians at Silistria—had agreed to place their army under his command. The implication was clear: the British army, numbering a mere 25,000 men, would play a minor part in the campaign compared to that played by the combined force of nearly 150,000 French and Turkish troops. In Paris, however, St. Arnaud had subscribed to the general view that the Turkish army was of little military value, a view that was also held in London. It was obvious that St. Arnaud's intention was to persuade Raglan that the allied armies would be more effective if they met the enemy together under one commander: St. Arnaud.

Raglan quietly rejected this naïve proposition. But St. Arnaud was not easily discouraged. He informed Raglan that, as no arrangements had been made in Paris about the command position if units of the two armies were to take the field side by side, he assumed that the joint command would automatically go to the senior officer present, whatever his nationality, and that the units would then fight as one. Since he was a marshal and outranked General Raglan, St. Arnaud would thus take over-all command whenever the two armies met the enemy together in battle—as was to be the case at the Alma.

To counter these blatant attempts by St. Arnaud to usurp command, Raglan had been obliged to enlist the help of de Redcliffe, the British ambassador at Constantinople. Fortunately de Redcliffe was able to produce a copy of the treaty that had been signed by Britain and France when they decided to go to war in support of Turkey. It had been stated clearly enough in the treaty that each commander was responsible solely to his own government and was to exercise independent command of all the men in his own army, whatever the circumstances.

Despite this unmasking of his intentions, St. Arnaud seemed in no way abashed, and he and Raglan did at last confer, in apparent cordiality, at Raglan's headquarters at Scutari. Raglan received the Marshal with his habitual charm and refrained from controversial discussion. At the time, the siege of Silistria was still going on, and there was no reason to believe that the Russians would not finally reduce the fortress, after which the road to Constantinople would be open. So the commanders agreed to move their armies to Varna, the port most accessible to Silistria, on the Black Sea coast. From here they could move to help the Turks when the situation at Silistria became dire.

After this agreement was made, St. Arnaud—in the manner of Louis Napoleon who, despite his ambition, was always apt to become frightened at the last moment—tried to depart from it by sending most of the French army to an entirely different and new position in Bulgaria, away from the coast and comfortably protected by a range of mountains from any possible contact with the Russians. It was only after Raglan's quiet insistence on St. Arnaud's honoring the agreement with which he himself had already complied, by sending the first of his units to Varna, that the French joined the British.

The British moved to Varna toward the end of May, and it was at this stage, when the first troops arrived and there still seemed to be no immediate prospect of fighting, that a few of the more adventurous young officers made their way surreptitiously to Silistria, some sixty miles away. (The others were only too happy to remain at Varna, where they found some excellent duck shooting.)

The French came early in June, bringing cholera with them, and for the next two months the allied armies suffered worse privation and heavier casualties than if they had been in constant battle. Without proper medical attention, the cholera victims suffered indescribably. The men who could still stand were kept working almost continuously as burial parties. The scourge spread to the allied fleets assembled in Balchick Bay, a few miles north of Varna, and because the authorities were convinced that the cholera germs had a local origin and were borne on Bulgarian breezes, many of the ships were sent out to sea to escape contagion. There they became death traps as the scourge ravaged the crowded lower decks where sailors herded themselves together to avoid the offshore winds. One ship, H.M.S. *Britannia*, was at sea for only three days when 400 men came down with cholera, of whom over a hundred died. The bodies of the dead were thrown over the side with little more than token rites. In the few weeks before the British and French armies left Bulgaria, they suffered more than 10,000 casualties, without even so much as skirmishing with the Russians.

It hardly seems credible that—after the siege of Silistria had been raised, the Russians had withdrawn from Guirgevo, and hostilities had seemed virtually finished—either the French or the British would go out of their way to find a pretext for continuing the war, yet St. Arnaud took three infantry divisions from Varna on a forced march of a hundred miles into Bulgarian territory, hoping to catch the Russians in retreat and thereby gain some of the credit for having rid Turkey of the Russian menace. He told Lord Raglan nothing of his intention, although the two commanders had set up neighboring headquarters at Varna. St. Arnaud's force made no contact with the Russians, but during the expedition 3,000 of his soldiers died of cholera.

In England there was a clamorous war party that had convinced the public that the only way to an "honorable peace" was to capture and destroy the symbol of Russian power in the Black Sea, the naval base at Sebastopol—an objective that became an end in itself, overriding all rational consideration of its relevance to the real issues. For when the British army had been sent away in the spring, Sebastopol was in the public mind as the definitive target of the war. Now that the Russian advance was halted, there was clearly no alternative to the destruction of the naval base.

That the naval base had strategic value could not be denied. It was not so evident that the western powers would achieve any strategic advantage to themselves merely by capturing Sebastopol—or even the whole of the Crimea—and saddling themselves with a continuing commitment to help the Turks keep it. But this does not seem to have been considered, even in the highest quarters. Louis Napoleon was ready to follow Britain blindly, so long as her way led to military glory. The British Prime Minister, Lord Aberdeen, had all along declared himself averse to war; he had said repeatedly that Britain had no intention of being drawn into it. His pacific declarations only encouraged the Tsar to adopt an aggressive attitude toward Turkey. Had Aberdeen made it clear that Britain really intended to fight, the Tsar most likely would have demurred and there might have been no Crimean War.

By now the British cabinet was dominated by the war faction, led by Lord Palmerston, and when the news came that the Russians had withdrawn from the Danube, a dispatch was sent to Lord Raglan instructing him to embark on the siege of Sebastopol. The dispatch certainly gave Raglan some discretion in deciding whether or not to comply with his instructions, but the discretion was so circumscribed that it was virtually impossible for him not to follow orders. As one of his divisional generals remarked, the government was clearly determined on the invasion, and if Raglan was not prepared to undertake it he would only be replaced by some other general. Louis Napoleon was content to fall in with whatever was decided by his influential allies, and he instructed Marshal St. Arnaud to take his army to the Crimea if Raglan decided to go there.

So, without any consideration of the strategic or tactical problems involved, Raglan was committed to take his army to attack a Russian force in the Crimea the strength and disposition of which he had no knowledge of whatever. Estimates of Russian strength in the Crimea varied from 45,000 to 140,000, which indicates the abysmal paucity of allied intelligence. Although Sebastopol was a naval base, there was no suggestion that it should be attacked from the sea. Even the most sanguine agreed that it was far too heavily defended for such an attack to be contemplated.

Added to the problem of how the actual attack on Sebastopol was to be launched was the more immediate problem of how to invade the Crimea itself. As it turned out, the invasion was accomplished by a series of improvisations. Each step was thought out only after the one before it had been completed.

The armies were embarked and transported from Varna across the Black Sea in a motley armada of fighting ships and merchant vessels, and were landed on the Crimea at a point that was chosen only when the ships anchored off the western tip of the Crimean peninsula. On this occasion it was Raglan who acted without St. Arnaud, for the French commander was laid low by a chronic sickness which of late was incapacitating him more frequently and from which in fact he was to die in less than two weeks. Having sailed past the actual entrance to Sebastopol harbor, quite close inshore, and having examined the whole of the western coastline and the rugged shores round Cape Kherson, near the southern tip of the peninsula, but still lacking any precise knowledge of the geography inland, Raglan chose a stretch of open beach some thirty miles north of Sebastopol. It was the only beach along the whole of that part of the coast not dominated by high cliffs. Near the southern end of the beach was a ruined fort, and the point where the allies landed was always afterwards referred to as the Old Fort.

Raglan believed, with some justification, that the guns of the British and French fleets could outrange any field artillery that the Russians might be able to muster, and he felt confident that he could cover a landing so long as it was not overlooked by high ground. There were thirty ships of the line standing within half a mile of the shore, and collectively they mounted some 3,000 heavy-caliber pieces—mostly 32-pounders, throwing a ball six and a half inches in diameter. As the ships were anchored in three lines, not more than one-sixth of the guns could be brought to bear on the landing beach; even so, some 500 guns could come into simultaneous action. Naval guns were still smoothbore, as rifling of barrels had not yet progressed beyond small arms, but the extreme range of the heavier guns was 2,000 yards in the most favorable conditions of sea and wind (wind resistance has an appreciable effect on spherical shot). By the time a projectile reached that extreme range, however, its velocity was seriously reduced, and it was only traveling at about one-third of the speed at which it had left the muzzle of the gun. The Russians had some 32-pounders in their forts at Sebastopol (when the allies came to the position on the Alma they found a battery of fourteen such pieces facing them from an emplacement that came to be known as the Great Redoubt). But the ordinary field guns which the Russians might have brought down to oppose the landing

[29]

would have been 18-pounders at the most, with a high-trajectory range of no more than 1,000 yards.

The beach Raglan chose was ideal—it was sheer luck that there was such a beach on the coast at all—for it ran along a narrow spit of land behind which was a large salt-water lake. Thus the landing was protected from direct assault in front and by the fleet's guns in the rear. Nevertheless the troops on landing would have found themselves in a dangerous situation had the Russians made determined assaults at either end of the beach, for those directing the ships' guns would have been inhibited to some extent by fear of firing on their own troops.

The British and French armies came ashore in a procession of landing boats in what amounted to an exercise; they even relied on the sailors to carry them bodily the last few yards to dry land, if the boats did not actually touch the beach, for the British at least were so encumbered by their impractical uniforms that wading was almost impossible. However, the whole invasion force landed on enemy territory without a shot being fired to oppose it; five days later the armies were to set off on the southward march that was to bring them to the banks of the Alma.

4

MARCH TO THE ALMA

WHEN THE BRITISH and French armies landed on the Crimean peninsula in September 1854 they were still beset by cholera. Although the height of the epidemic had passed some weeks earlier, before they had sailed from Bulgaria, the germs were still present and men were still being struck down suddenly and terrifyingly, so that no one, no matter how well he seemed, could be sure that the dreadful sickness would not rise without any warning and kill him in a few hours' time. The French suffered most severely—10,000 French soldiers had died in little over a month—and on the voyage across the Black Sea one wretched victim after another, sewn up in his own blanket, had been thrown overboard. The British had lost at least 800 men. Now, with the two armies on Russian soil and likely to become heavily engaged in battle very soon, the disease was still taking its toll.

The landing of 65,000 men, with guns, horses, and equipment, took nearly five days to complete. The late summer days were still hot and most of the time the sky was cloudless. Even though a cool breeze blew in from the sea, the surf seldom hampered the landings, which were carried off with relatively little hardship. Once the armies were ashore, however, short-comings in organization were soon apparent. Although the French forces—commanded as they were by men for whom soldiering was a career—were generally better organized than those of the British, the beachhead as a whole was a scene of great confusion.

The British tents had been stored in the more inaccessible parts of the ships, and when a storm broke that evening, the troops had no shelter. They passed the night as best they could, lying in pools of water on the ground with the rain pouring down upon them. The cold and the damp had their inevitable effect, and that night cholera claimed more than its usual number of victims. Fortunately, when morning came the sun shone brightly again and the sky was as cloudless as it had been the day before. As there was no fresh water to be found near the landing beach and the hot sun soon dried up most of the rain that had fallen during the night, leaving only muddy pools, the sappers hurriedly sank some inadequate wells. But the water they struck was brackish, and when, on the fifth day, the armies began their march to meet the enemy, the British soldiers' water bottles were half empty, and what water they did contain was all but undrinkable.

The plan of campaign, insofar as there was a plan, was to march south from the landing beach, along the coast, to the Russian naval base at Sebastopol, some thirty miles and five river crossings away. Fortunately for the invaders, the Russians had so far merely sent some Cossack scouts to keep their movements under observation—a handful of horsemen seen fleetingly against the skyline, usually in the early morning. At the time, the Russians' failure to dispute the landing suggested to the allied soldiers—and even to some officers of high rank—that the whole campaign was going to be easy. Even the generals, by the way they acted, seemed to discount the possibility that the enemy might be reticent in the hope of drawing the invaders into a trap.

And so, on September 19, 1854, the British and French armies climbed up from their beachhead onto that high, rolling plateau, 300 to 400 feet above sea level, of which so much of the Crimea consists. There were 30,000 men in the French army, infantry and artillerymen only; added to these, under the French general, were 9,000 Turks. The British army numbered 26,000—infantry, cavalry, and artillery—under their own commander in chief. As one enormous, concentrated task force, under two separate commands, these 65,000 men assembled and marched off along the edge of the high plateau, along the crest of the steep cliffs that fall away to the Black Sea shore.

The French army, with the Turks, marched on the right flank, along the line of cliffs; the British marched close on their left, on the inland flank. The French marched in four divisions, in a diamond formation—with the Turkish battalions enveloped in the center of the diamond—each division in two long brigade columns. There were five British divisions, four of which were grouped in a square—a formation known in those days as "grand divisions"—with the odd division bringing up the rear. Each British division marched in close column as one huge phalanx with a front and depth of at least a mile, so that the whole effect was of much greater concentration than that of the French forces. The difference in the formations of the two armies revealed their distinctive tactical philosophies: British reliance on the line and French insistence on the column. Should the enemy be encountered on the march, the British divisions could be readily deployed into line, facing either the front or the flank, while for their part the French would have to remain in their columns. That was how the two armies had

[33]

fought each other before in Europe; and now that they were allied in war, each army still fought the same way.

The British were resplendent in their brightly colored uniforms. By now, in all the European armies, the sort tunic and trousers had replaced those long-skirted coats and breeches that had been universal military wear for centuries. During the eighteenth century it had been the practice to loop up the skirts of the coat when they were not needed for protection from the weather, and that was how the shorter tunic had first developed. (It was only after coat-skirts were discarded that the need for overcoats arose.) In Britain, during the long peace after Waterloo, the tunic had grown shorter and shorter, as commanding officers developed their fanciful ideas of ceremonial dress. In many regiments it had now evolved into nothing more than a skin-tight long-sleeved vest—in bright-hued red or blue (in one regiment, green)—buttoned tightly at the throat, or else surmounted by an equally choking stock. To the tunics were sewn all sorts of gaudy gold and colored trimmings: buttons, facings, cuirasses, epaulettes, cuffs. The trousers were skin-tight too, often in a color different from that of the tunic, and they also had their assortments of gaudy stripes. Headdresses were multifarious—helmets, shakos, busbies, Glengarries, Highland bonnets, and, among the senior officers, gaily plumed cocked hats. The cavalry wore even more elaborate cuirasses, and some slung gorgeous pelisses over their shoulders —all these trimmings in vivid, brilliant colors.

In comparison, the French were almost drab in their dark blue tunics and trousers—a looser, more practicable and comfortable battle dress not far removed from that of modern times. There were, of course, the Zouaves, conspicuous in the French columns, in their loose vests and baggy breeches, with their bright cummerbunds—a uniform uniquely suitable for campaigns in the desert heat. (The Zouave regiments were no longer made up of native Arabs, as they had been when first formed during the Algerian campaign. They had been manned by French volunteers for the last two years, although this was the first time they had moved out of Algeria.)

Despite their concentration, the invaders covered a sizable area. The whole formation presented a front four miles wide and stretched three miles from van to rear. It was an entirely detached force, cut off on three sides by the empty plain and on the fourth by the sea, so that it composed twelve square miles of military might moving in complete and lonely isolation —except that, offshore, it was supported by the allied fighting ships, sailing slowly along the coast, parallel to the armies' line of march. The British had left in the rear a few companies of infantrymen with orders to clear up some of the disorder on the beach before reuniting with the main body. Once reunion took place, the isolation of the invading force would be complete. For there was no line of communication with the base; indeed, properly speaking there was no base.

Once again the sky was cloudless and the day promised to be hot, but in the early hours the breeze from the sea tempered the heat of the sun and the soldiers strode forward with deceptive ease over the coarse, matted grass of the plain. They started in high spirits, singing and calling to each other cheerfully, but before long all suggestion of gaiety disappeared; within a few hours, after repeated halts, the British army, at least, was trudging along in virtual silence, leaving behind a trail of exhausted, stricken men and discarded equipment. The effect was more of a spent army in retreat than of one advancing toward the first engagement in its campaign.

That afternoon the armies reached the first river crossing, the Bulganak. The ground fell gently down from the sloped plateau to the level of the stream and rose again from its south bank in a series of terraces. A column of 2,000 Russian cavalry-men was drawn up on one of the lower terraces; and higher up, almost hidden by an intervening ridge, and actually revealed only by the sunlight glinting on a mass of bayonets showing over the top of the ridge, stood a force of some 6,000 Russian infantry. The British advance guard—four cavalry squadrons, less than 300 men in all—had already crossed the stream and trotted up to the first ridge. Now it stood, extended into line, face to face with the Russian horsemen. At last, the allies and the Russians, who had declared war on each other six months ago and had yet to make contact, stood facing each other across a few hundred yards of empty grassland. The moment was dramatic enough, but the excitement dissolved almost im-mediately in an anticlimax. Lord Raglan, the British commander in chief, recalled his outnumbered cavalry, and the Russian force, faced with the obviously overwhelming superiority of two entire armies, withdrew over the ridges to the south. The only confirmation that a state of war existed between the great powers was the exchange of a few ineffective shots fired at random by the field guns of both sides.

But the allied soldiers had found ample water at last, and if at any time during the whole campaign in the Crimea the discipline of some units of the British army showed the slightest slackening, it was that afternoon on the Bulganak when not a few men broke ranks to satisfy their desperate thirst.

The Bulganak turned out to be little more than a shallow stream, which the armies crossed easily. But it was clear to the allied generals that they had come far enough for one day—although they had in fact marched less than eight miles—and so that night the allies bivouacked on the south bank of the Bulganak, with the British, on the open flank, disposed in order of battle, lest the Russians change their minds and return to launch an attack.

The night of September 19 gave the allies, particularly the British, a providential breathing spell. The day's march, comparatively short as it had been, disclosed much of the force's weakness, and now that the armies had come down to sea level again, for a brief time, they were able to make fresh contact with the ships and have those men who were obviously unfit to march and fight taken off by boat. Those who remained were refreshed by the cool water of the Bulganak as they had not been properly refreshed since they landed, although the stream was so muddied by the thousands of troops tramping across that it was not easy to draw fresh water that night.

The forward units of the armies, bivouacked at the top of the ridge, looked southward over the plateau, in the direction in which they were to continue their march next morning. There they could see the flicker of scores of small fires not more than a few miles away; and although the men in the allied armies, most of whom had never seen action, were profoundly ignorant of the intentions of their leaders and of the geography of the country they were invading, they could have no doubt that the fires marked the line where they would meet, and almost certainly have to fight, the enemy next day. That night there was less talk in the English army of an easy campaign, if only because the enemy was no longer the abstraction he had been for the past six months: he had now been seen in the flesh and his proximity in force was a tangible reality. When the army marched off next morning, it would be in a mood very different from the spirit of near irresponsibility in which it had set off twenty-four hours before. Not that the soldiers were anything but confident and in good heart. But a sense of purpose pervaded the ranks, virtually in a night, and the men were to march off quietly without any of the surface exuberance they had affected the previous day.

On that same evening, September 19, when the allied armies bivouacked on the banks of the Bulganak, Marshal St. Arnaud, the French commander in chief, rode across to the little post-house by the river bridge in which Lord Raglan had set up his headquarters and in which he was to sleep that night. The bridge was part of the main road that ran parallel with the coast and connected Sebastopol with Eupatoria, a town a few miles north of the beach on which the allies had landed. It was a good road: from Eupatoria it ran south along the spit of land that separates the salt lake from the landing beach; then it rose onto the plain, dipping down as it came to each river valley. Strong wooden bridges carried it over the Bulganak, the Alma, the Katcha, and the Belbek, and finally it ran around the head of Sebastopol harbor and crossed the Tchernaya River over a low bridge before entering the harbor itself. As they marched over the plain, the armies generally followed the direction of the road; but for a force that stretched out across a front nearly four miles wide, in completely open country, the exact position of the road was unimportant.

Since the armies had landed, St. Arnaud had temporarily recovered from his sickness, and that evening he came to Raglan's headquarters by the bridge, apparently in high spirits. He was accompanied by a Colonel Trochu whom he always passed off as his chief of staff, but it was clear enough to Raglan and his colleagues that Trochu had in fact been sent by the Emperor to keep a restraining hand on St. Arnaud's tendency towards rash enterprise.

The irrepressible Marshal clearly had some notion that he was determined to impose on Raglan. In deference to the

British general he tried to present his proposal in English, but he was so excited and vehement that he kept losing the thread of his thoughts, and in the long monologue into which he launched he alternated between English and French. It remained a monologue, because from the outset Raglan showed no inclination to contribute any remark so long as St. Arnaud went on talking. Raglan, amiable as ever, seemed to listen attentively enough, giving the impression that he was assenting to what St. Arnaud was saying, but those present at the scene remarked later than his main concern seemed to have been to hide his amusement at the sheer artlessness of St. Arnaud's proposals.

There was unspoken agreement that the Russians would be waiting for the allies when they reached the Alma next day, and that there the first—perhaps decisive—battle would be fought. Neither Raglan nor St. Arnaud seemed to doubt that this first battle would actually be on the line of the Alma, although they never discussed the matter. There was, of course, the danger that the Russians might attack the exposed flank of the British army, bivouacked on the Bulganak, during the night, and Raglan had made special dispositions on this account. But even if they were to do this, the attack would be unlikely to result in a full-scale battle. It was unthinkable that the Russians would commit their main army in the dark.

There was also the possibility that they might attack early next morning, or that instead of waiting on the Alma they might take the initiative and attack on the flank while the allies were still on the march. Skilfully handled, such a flank attack, combined with a movement against the allies' rear, could be overwhelming. Between rivers, cut off from their ships by unscalable cliffs, the allied armies could be virtually encircled; the ships' guns would be able to do little to interfere with a main Russian attack launched three or four miles inland. Only after the allies were driven into a corner on the edge of the cliffs would the guns be of any help, and then they would be too late. A beleaguered force, with no reinforcements within a thousand miles and cut off entirely from any source of supply, the allied armies would soon use up their food and water.

So it was not necessarily a certainty that the battle would be joined on the banks of the Alma, although neither commander suggested that anything else might occur. What limited discussion they had was based on the comfortable belief that their forces would reach the Alma River undisturbed and there the Russians would be waiting for them in a straightforward line stretching from east to west.

There was some evidence to support this belief at the time, although it was not overwhelming. No attempt had been made to send out scouts to ascertain the enemy positions; perhaps, due to the open country, this was not very practical in any case. But some of the French ships had sailed along the coast and reconnoitered the mouth of the Alma, where they could see fairly clearly the positions taken up by the Russians along the hills rising from the south bank of the river. Not that what they could see necessarily comprised the whole Russian army: the oblique view from the river mouth made it difficult to scrutinize the positions in any detail beyond a couple of miles, even with the strongest glasses; and in any case the river took a bend to the northeast three miles from its mouth. There might well have been a strong force deployed higher upstream on the north bank, waiting to attack the allies on the flank. Nobody had any knowledge of the strength of the Russian armies in the Crimea, and the troops that could be seen along the river bank might have been only a portion of the whole force.

There was, however, one valuable item of intelligence of

which the ships had been able to make certain, and that was that there were no Russian forces on the slopes rising from the south bank for at least a mile or more upriver; nor were there any Russians on the cliffs overlooking the river mouth. The Russians had left this sector uncovered because apparently they were satisfied that these slopes and cliffs were unassailable, but the sailors had spotted what appeared to be a relatively easy path leading up from the beach at the river mouth, and they had also found a sand bar that seemed to make the river easily fordable.

On the strength of this intelligence, St. Arnaud had concocted his *Projet pour la bataille de l'Alma*. He had sketched this plan on a rough sheet of paper, although, like Raglan, he had no idea of any of the tactical features of the ground on which the battle was likely to be fought. The course of the river itself was indicated merely by a wavy line, which indeed approximated the direction that the river took inland but showed none of the sharp bends and loops that were to become so important to the soldiers. To the south of the river he had sprinkled on the plan a series of small squares and broken lines marked *Redoute* and *Position des Russes* which were based on no intelligence of where the actual Russian positions or earthworks were likely to be; nor did his plan indicate where there were plantations or buildings that could provide cover; how the hills rose from the river bank; where the slopes were gradual and where they were steep; where there were any roads or paths leading up their face; or even whether it was possible to ascend the hills at all. The truth is, of course, that St. Arnaud did not know any of this information. But thanks to the report from the ships of a possible way up the cliffs, he had been able to insert on the plan one specific reference to a tactical movement—even if it was the only one

[4 1]

—by showing the planned movement of two divisions, *Division Turque* and *Division Bosquet,* toward the mouth of the river at five o'clock in the morning. (In actual fact he was wrong to label these as two divisions; General Bosquet's was certainly a full division complete with guns—the 2nd Division—but the Turks comprised only a number of independent battalions.)

Right across the center of the position on the allied side of the river, St. Arnaud had shown the whole French army deployed in line—quite out of character—at whose head he had placed an arrow pointing at the heart of the Russian positions. On the opposite flank from *Division Bosquet*—that is to say, on the left of the French army—the British were represented by five indefinitely sketched lines, each with an arrow suggesting a turning movement, the whole labeled *Armée anglaise tournant la droite ennemie* and hopefully annotated *Départ à 5h½*. The British seemed to be shown, equally uncharacteristically, as attacking in columns.

The tactics suggested by the plan were clear enough. Bosquet's division was to cross the river at its mouth and engage the enemy's left, while the whole British army was to turn the enemy's right by swinging around the other flank—where, incidentally, the allies knew nothing of the strength and disposition of the Russian forces or even of the ground that would have to be fought over. Meanwhile the French army would advance en masse on the center of the Russian position, and play the principal part in the Battle of the Alma. (After the battle was fought, this plan reached France and was published in the French press, quite mendaciously, as what actually took place at the Alma.)

These were the proposals that St. Arnaud was now commending to Raglan with such vehemence. It is not surprising that Raglan found it difficult to hide his amusement. Nor is it surprising that, although St. Arnaud was commanding the army of one of the world's greatest military powers, he was unable to produce anything less jejune. Had it not been that Louis Napoleon wanted him for a special purpose, he would have remained an undistinguished officer—an old soldier from whom nobody would have expected anything beyond the routine. Although he may have been able to command a brigade against Algerian tribesmen, he had no conception of what was involved in a full-scale army battle. However, he had convinced himself of the merit of his plan and he described to Raglan, with all his Gallic vehemence and not a little pantomime, the effect of Bosquet's probe on the enemy's left and the overwhelming French attack on his front.

Raglan showed St. Arnaud an almost exaggerated attentiveness but made no comment. He merely volunteered, because he did not wish to appear impolite, that St. Arnaud could rely on the co-operation of the British army, so when the Marshal left he believed that Raglan had accepted the plan and intended to follow it. Even so, it was a little sanguine of St. Arnaud to expect—as he apparently did—that Raglan, who had heard nothing of the plan before, would now arrange for the whole British army to be redeployed in five divisional columns and be on the move in a newly projected direction by half-past five in the morning.

No attempt was made by either commander to go into any detail. The only item touched on during the discussion was raised by Trochu, who asked St. Arnaud when he intended to order the French soldiers to lay down their packs. It was a practice in the French army for the soldiers to discard their heavy packs before engaging in battle, and until they received the order to drop their packs they were reluctant to commit themselves to combat.

[43]

St. Arnaud felt that reference to such a trivial detail was out of place in a high-level discussion on tactical policy, and he dismissed Trochu's question with some impatience. Then he took leave of the British general, his good spirits in no way diminished, and rode with Trochu back to the French lines. Raglan retired that night without making any special dispositions for the next morning.

The British soldier of those days was not an early riser. Whereas in modern warfare actions are usually launched between midnight and dawn, so that by the time the sun is up the soldier's day is well advanced, in the old days the British liked to finish their breakfast before they started any fighting. The officers, particularly, were influenced by the habits of their normal social lives; even on active service they were wont to indulge in extensive toilets, so they were seldom available for duty before seven or eight o'clock and preferred that the day start at nine. In this they differed conspicuously from the more professional French. On the previous day, when the armies had started off on the first stage of their march, the intention had been to get under way early. Reveille had been sounded in both camps at three o'clock, but it had taken the British until nine to complete their preparations, and for two or three hours preceding departure the French had repeatedly proclaimed their impatience by bugling and drumming.

On that first day the British army had marched in its "grand divisions" and would continue its march next morning in the same formation. But during the night, while the armies rested on the Bulganak, the British divisions were deployed in a different formation. The two forward divisions were moved across to the left flank and extended in a line running at an oblique angle to the rest of the army. This line followed the course of the river, which bent to the northeast some three miles inland.

When morning came, the two divisions had to be brought back to the line of march—the movement of each involving two complicated wheels made by 5,000 men in close formation.

These maneuvers, involving large bodies of troops moving over uneven ground, were quite beyond the regimental officers, who had no experience of moving anything but small formations across nicely rolled barrack squares. Thanks to the training and discipline of the soldiers themselves, the movements were eventually completed, but they literally took hours.

Moreover, although the armies had landed with no transport, they had managed to intercept a convoy of carts on the road from Eupatoria carrying supplies for the Russians, and some allied raiding parties had requisitioned more farm carts from nearby Tatar villages. All together they had collected more than 300 vehicles, such as they were—rough pole frames on wooden axles, drawn by bullocks. The Tatar drivers had been impressed into the allies' service, not altogether unwillingly, and the carts had been loaded with barrels of pork, cases of biscuits, and, more importantly, with the precious supply of reserve ammunition. To protect his army's carts during the night, Raglan had moved them from their position in the order of march and placed them between the flank divisions and the river, so that when the line was resumed next morning they had to be dragged back again—at bullock speed.

Altogether, the process of re-forming the line of march was protracted and vexatious. Sir George Brown, the general commanding the British Light Division, knew that the march was to resume at seven, but in the morning he waited calmly in his tent until the order was specifically repeated. Actually his division did not start its redeployment until nearly nine o'clock. Sir George had fought at Corunna forty-six years before, and his age hardly inclined him to hurry. In addition, he firmly believed that his soldiers should be immaculate, whatever the circumstances, and he had them flogged without compunction when they were not; so his regimental officers needed plenty of time to make their routine inspection. His colleague commanding the 2nd Division, Sir George de Lacy Evans, was sixty-seven and had fought in the Peninsula campaign too—and was equally averse to undignified haste—so Marshal St. Arnaud miscalculated the probabilities when he proposed that the British divisions should be on the move by half-past five.

It was half-past five when General Bosquet, with the French 2nd Division and the Turkish battalions, started his move, quietly and efficiently. Usually the French announced all their comings and goings by loud bugling and rolling of drums, but St. Arnaud was optimistic enough to believe that by some miracle he was going to surprise the Russians, and he had ordered the army to move quietly in the morning. Quietness is, of course, a relative thing. Any movement of an army is accompanied by unavoidable uproar, but as the enemy was still three miles away only the more strident noises would be likely to reach him. As it happened, Bosquet's division moved away unadvertised, although later in the morning its stealth did not count for much; it could plainly be seen waiting on the edge of the cliffs.

The key to St. Arnaud's plan was to take advantage of the absence of enemy troops at the river mouth, and he wanted to conceal from the Russians, as long as he could, his intention of sending a force to attack them on that flank. But after Bosquet and his men had been moving in close column along the edge of the cliffs for nearly an hour, they could see that the rest of the French army, which had started to march off in their wake soon after six o'clock, had halted. It looked as if the delay was to be protracted, because the French soldiers could be seen settling down to make coffee, and Bosquet had perforce to wait too. The French were, in fact, waiting for their allies to get under way.

The British divisions were still making their complicated wheels. They found that their whole army was obliged to swing around through a wide arc, because the line of coast running towards the Alma struck out at an angle from the line of the Bulganak, and the actual direction of march varied by some twenty degrees from the front that the two armies had faced on their line of bivouac during the night. So, in addition to redeploying the Light and 2nd Divisions and bringing the supply carts back into position, the British army, once it got under way, had to wheel again to the right—a maneuver that involved marching more than a mile farther than the French, who, in their column formation on the inside flank, had been able to set off in the new direction without any intricate movement.

The British army did not initially wheel through a wide enough arc. Consequently, as the march continued, the two armies, which had lost touch when the French moved off early in the morning, grew progressively farther apart. The British halted again, and there followed once more the complicated business of forming and wheeling—still almost beyond the capacity of the regimental officers—until finally the divisions were moved over far enough to the right to restore contact with the French army. Then it was found that the British front had come in line with Bosquet's division, so now it was the turn of the French to move forward while the British were held back. It was not until half-past eleven, six hours after Bosquet had made his first hopeful move, that the British and French armies were properly aligned in their order of march.

[47]

Less than three miles from the Bulganak, the leading files came to a ridge from which the high ground again fell gently down to sea level. Then it rose in a series of steep hills that stood out so sharply from the landscape that from the north they looked almost like a wall. Spaced along the upper levels of the hills could be seen the massed formations of a considerable army. Here was a formidable natural barrier in the line of the allies' southward march, and here was the Russian army disposed to exploit it.

The grass on the plain had been bleached nearly white by the hot summer sun, and where there was no grass the earth was dusty and brown. The face of the hills to the south showed bare brown patches; the only dark places to be seen on them were the massed Russian columns. But along the foot of the hills, from east to west, ran a belt of verdant green, relieving the arid effect of the dusty plain and the brown hills —cypresses and willows, gardens and vineyards, and a couple of colorful little hamlets nestling in the trees. The allied soldiers, halted on the crest of the northern slope, could see sparkling through the trees a silver streak of water running out to sea.

They had come to the Alma River at last.

It was shortly after noon when the armies halted. Due to a conjunction of circumstances, complete silence settled over the armies as they came to a halt. It was a silence that might well have been staged by an imaginative Providence intent on exploiting the drama of the situation: here, after months of uncertainty, the armies of the great European powers stood face to face.

Every man on the field that day noticed the stillness because it was so incongruous, and many remembered afterwards that it was made even more pronounced by little disconnected sounds that interrupted but failed to break it—someone striking his musket against a ration tin; a horse neighing—so that, insignificant as each sound was, thousands of men turned to see whence it came.

The silence was finally broken when Sir Colin Campbell, who commanded the Highland Brigade, said quietly—although many heard him—"This will be a good time for the men to get loose half their cartridges."

The armies seemed to come to life again. The Highlanders opened their packets of cartridges and shook a number loose, ready for action. The order was repeated through the brigades and the battalions and the companies, and soon the armies were clattering and clanking again and the strange silence ended. It was high noon, like a hot summer's day in England. Although many throats were dry, most soldiers were carefully preserving the water in their bottles, having been warned by those few in the ranks who knew anything of battles at first hand that before the day was out they might be gasping for even a few drops.

Marshal St. Arnaud, preceded by a trooper carrying his guidon, rode across the front of his army toward the British lines. Raglan went to meet him, and together the two commanders rode forward onto a low mound that broke the almost level surface of the plain. In full view of their armies, and of the enemy, they spoke together for some minutes, each raising his telescope to examine the Russian positions; Raglan could be seen showing St. Arnaud how a support had been rigged up on his saddle to help him manipulate his telescope with his only hand.

It must have been clear by now to St. Arnaud that Raglan had no intention of falling in with the plan he had proposed the night before. The British army, far from filing away to the left in a series of columns, was spread out just as widely across the center of the position as the French army; while not yet extended into line, it covered a formidable front nevertheless. St. Arnaud had put his own part of the plan into motion by sending Bosquet forward, but he was inhibited from making his next move by the British army's occupation of most of the ground across which he had intended to deploy the French.

It is difficult not to feel sorry for St. Arnaud as it became clear to him that Raglan had completely ignored his proposal. Nobody could hear what was going on between the two men, but from their manner they seemed to be viewing the scene more like casual tourists than generals debating a plan for action. Raglan was clearly exercising his usual amiable charm; and his colleagues could realize he was doing his best to deflect St. Arnaud's attempts to make him commit himself. General Airey, the British Quartermaster General—a position which in those days was equivalent to chief of staff—rode forward to join the two commanders. As he came within earshot, he heard St. Arnaud asking, almost in exasperation, whether Raglan intended to turn the position or attack in front.

St. Arnaud received the answer that told him his plan had been discarded. Raglan looked out over the enemy lines toward his left and said, "With such a body of cavalry as the enemy has on the plain, I would not attempt to turn the position." Of what he might intend to do as an alternative, he gave no indication.

Nothing more was said, and the tactics the two armies were to follow during the next few hours were left entirely in the air.

It was now one o'clock, and, while the commanders still sat their horses on the mound, bugles sounded and the British army started to move forward again in accordance with orders that had obviously already been given. St. Arnaud, bewildered and feeling not a little slighted, took leave of Raglan and rode back toward his own lines, where he called together his divisional generals. He allowed Bosquet to continue moving forward on the flank, and the French 2nd Division, with the Turkish battalions, started to make its way down the diminishing cliffs to the mouth of the Alma River.

5

RUSSIANS ON THE HILLS

Without being planned to do so, the allied landing on the Crimean peninsula completely surprised the Russians, who were utterly unprepared to put up any resistance. They soon realized, however, that the invading armies would march south to Sebastopol. Here, in command, was Prince Menshikov, the emasculated general sent by the Tsar to bully the Turks in Constantinople, prior to the declaration of war. The first decision which Menshikov had to make when he learned of the landing was whether to wait for the invaders' assault on the town or go out and challenge them on the approach march.

There were two routes which the allies could take from the Old Fort to Sebastopol. One was their actual route, astride the coastal road that followed the shoreline southward until it crossed the Belbek and then swung in around the head of Sebastopol harbor. But another road struck southeastward from the Old Fort to Bakshiserai, fifteen miles inland (and joined a third road that ran across the heart of the peninsula and connected Sebastopol with both the mainland to the north and the Kerch peninsula to the east). There might not have been much advantage to the allies if they had taken this second road; it would have involved a longer march, they would have found Bakshiserai occupied by Russian troops, and the final approach to Sebastopol would have been from the same direction. Nevertheless, the allies might well have decided to split their forces and send one army by each route; that way, they could have imposed on the Russians an intricate problem of defense; assuming the Russians came out from Sebastopol to meet them, the allies could not have failed to profit from the confusion they would have caused. Consequently, Menshikov had first to find out by which route or routes the allies were marching, and it was for this purpose that he had sent out his reconnaissance in force to the Bulganak on September 19.

When Menshikov learned that the allies were marching unimaginatively in one concentrated force straight down the coastal route, he decided—with equal lack of imagination—to bar their progress at the Alma River, and he hurriedly brought out most of the troops in Sebastopol.

The line of the Alma River was not an acknowledged position, already prepared for defense. Sebastopol was a heavily garrisoned town that should have been ready to meet any attack. Its defense was now improvised, within a few hours, by moving the defenders to a totally unprepared position fifteen miles away.

Menshikov—who, to do him justice, had taken over command in the town only a few weeks before—was faced with the difficulty that no preparations had been made to guard against the possibility of an assault on Sebastopol from the north. The harbor was well protected by forts at its entrance, and a new fort, the Star Fort, had been built quite recently on the crest of the high ground that rose from the northern shore at the harbor mouth. The Star Fort looked imposing enough on the skyline, to anyone climbing up from the Belbek River to approach Sebastopol from the north, but all its guns pointed the other way, southwest, towards the harbor mouth. There was no other physical obstacle in the way of a force bearing down on the northern shore of the harbor.

Before setting foot in the town, an enemy attacking Sebastopol from the north would obviously have to cross the wide reach of harbor. This was a serious obstacle, but it was not necessarily insurmountable, particularly if a diversion were made by ships attacking the harbor entrance and drawing off the Russian warships lying in the basin. In any case, the assault would be brought right to the edge of the town—a development that Menshikov decided, at the eleventh hour, to avoid at all cost.

So, quite empirically, he set about improvising a line between the town and the advancing invaders. He gave no thought to the possibility of striking the allied armies on their flank; with his lack of tactical perception, he could think of nothing to do except impose his own forces as a static obstacle in their path. He would wait for the allies to do the attacking, and his army would resist the attack. It never occurred to him that every mile the allies moved southward increased the vulnerability of their position and invited the Russians to encircle them. Nor did he appear to realize that if, by an imaginative use of this opportunity they were giving him, he were to take the initiative and close them in a trap, he would no longer be the timorous defender of Sebastopol but, by going over to the offensive himself, would have the allies fighting for their lives.

Since Menshikov was not a tactician, a war of movement was beyond his perception. Nevertheless, if he had to choose

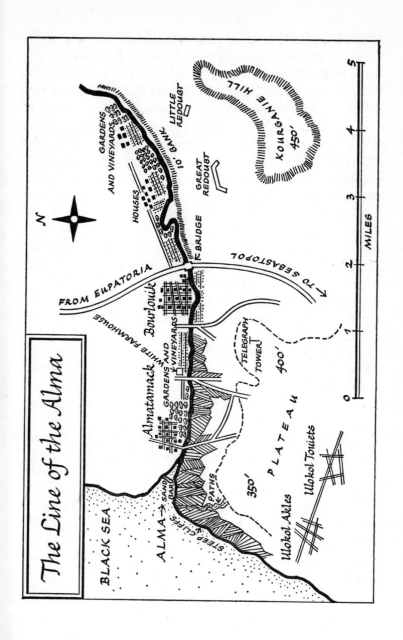

The Line of the Alma

a position on which to meet the allies on the march, he could not have chosen better than the heights rising from the south bank of the Alma River. But his ignorance of the ground on which he set up his line of defense, and the ill-conceived way in which he placed the forces at his disposal, both confirm that the whole exercise was nothing more than an improvisation. His choice of the Alma was elementary enough, because the hills rising from the other rivers are not nearly as steep. But that fact seems to have been the extent of his knowledge of the local topography. Neither he nor his three subordinate generals made any detailed examination of the ground, and in the hurried twenty-four hours after the decision was made to stop the allies on the Alma, Menshikov, simply feeling his way, disposed the Russian formations with little reference to the tactical realities of the situation. In particular, he made no attempt to occupy the cliffs overlooking the mouth of the river, because, in his ignorance of the ground, he firmly believed them to be unassailable.

It is true that, for the first two miles upriver, the cliffs rising from the south bank are uncommonly steep and virtually unscalable. They rise almost vertically to a plateau 350 feet above the level of the river. There was, of course, the path which the French ships had spotted, winding up the face of the cliffs where they turn to overlook the shore at the river mouth. On the north bank, a mile upstream, was a village called Almatamack, a cluster of peasants' houses marking the lower end of the vineyards and gardens that lined the river for some miles. A ford crossed the river at Almatamack, and a road solid enough even for guns ran from the ford into a ravine that wound its way up to the top of the cliffs on the south bank. Here was another easy means of access to the plateau, but Menshikov ignored it entirely and left it undefended.

Admittedly, the open plateau at the top of the cliffs is within range of the guns of any ships lying offshore. But any gunnery brought to bear in those days could not have been very effective, because the plateau is 350 feet above sea level and the guns would have had to be fired at their highest elevation. Moreover, except along the edge of the cliffs, any specific target would be out of the gunners' sight. There were no spotting aids to gunnery in the mid-nineteenth century; if the gunner could not actually see his target, the shooting was wild and generally ineffective. Menshikov did post a battalion of infantry and a pair of his own guns at a little village, Ulukol Akles, at the top of the cliffs to the south, a mile away from the river. But in that direction the ground fell away slightly, so these troops were stationed below the crest of the plateau and could see nothing of the river itself, nor could they see the northern slopes on the other side of the river, down which the allied armies were marching.

The sheer cliffs continue upriver for a couple of miles. The road from the ford at Almatamack, on reaching the top, turned to run along the crest of the cliffs, parallel with the river. At a point nearly a mile above the ford, another road found its way up a ravine. This second road would not take guns, nor was there another ford at the point where it ran down to the river. Although it presented an easy way for any infantry that might manage to cross the river to gain the top of the plateau, Menshikov again left it undefended.

Two and a half miles from the river mouth the sheer cliffs give way to hills, receding from the river as they rise from the bank. Nevertheless, they rise just as high as the cliffs, up to the level of the plateau, and at two points they rise to more than 400 feet. This plateau came to be known as the Telegraph Height, because at the time of the battle an unfinished tower had been erected on it to carry a telegraph installation—not an electric telegraph, but the arms of a visual semaphore in a line of relay signal stations along the coast. The faces of the slopes rising from the riverbank to the Telegraph Height are very steep, although not as sheer as the cliffs downriver, but they are cut with gullies and ravines, and there were four usable roads that found their way to the top. It was at this point, on a ledge that ran beside the river channel at the foot of these hills, that Menshikov started his line of defensive positions, which extended upstream for another three miles— although they were not actually continued along the riverbank itself. Thus, in essence, Menshikov left the first two miles of the Alma heights undefended, because he believed they were unassailable, and took his stand against the advancing allies farther upstream, on a comparatively narrow three-mile front.

A little higher up the river from these first hills—as distinct from the sheer cliffs—the road to Sebastopol crossed by a strong wooden bridge. Downstream from the bridge, as far as the ford crossing from Almatamack more than two miles away, there is a flat ledge almost on the water level, between the foot of the hills and the winding channel of the river itself. The width of the ledge varies, because the line of hills is comparatively straight while the river takes a number of sharp bends. At some points it is only 200 yards wide, at others its width is nearly a quarter of a mile. There were some vineyards planted on this ledge, and they ran for nearly a mile below the bridge, the only cultivated stretch on the south bank.

Above the bridge, the ledge continues along the south bank, but it is only a few yards wide. Here, for at least two miles upriver, the hills that run down from the southern heights— although they are not nearly as steep as those below the bridge

[58]

—drop abruptly to this narrow ledge, leaving a sheer vertical bank ten to fifteen feet high. Atop this miniature cliff the ground rises more gradually than anywhere else along Menshikov's position, and a mile away from the riverbank it sweeps up to a high spur, the Kourganie Hill, the highest feature in the line of hills running beside the Alma valley. The crest of the hill is more than 450 feet high, and the hill runs for a mile almost due east and west—at an angle to the line of the river which swings northeastward just above the bridge. The sides of Kourganie Hill drop steeply from its crest and then, for the last half-mile down to the little cliffs above the river bank, flatten out to comparatively gentle slopes.

Menshikov chose Kourganie Hill as the center of his defensive position, and he disposed most of his forces around it. On the slopes running down toward the river, he constructed his only prepared fieldworks. First, he dug a shallow breastwork, not more than 300 yards long, parallel with the river and about 600 yards from it. The earthwork was to contain fourteen heavy guns which he had brought from Sebastopol—32-pounders and 24-pound howitzers. In subsequent descriptions of the battle this earthwork is always called the Great Redoubt, if only to distinguish it from the Lesser Redoubt, which was a similar but shorter trench containing a battery of field guns. The Lesser Redoubt was placed higher up Kourganie Hill, a mile to the east, and it ran at right angles to the line of river to cover the Russian right flank. Nowhere else on the whole Alma line did the Russians dig so much as a trench. Wherever else Menshikov disposed his battalions, they stood—or lay down—upon the open faces of the hills, or in some instances they waited behind the cover of convenient hollows in the ground.

Menshikov had brought from Sebastopol to the Alma

39,000 troops: 33,000 infantry, 3,400 cavalry, and 2,600 artillerymen with 106 guns. The Russian units were, for the most
part, conventional battalions of regiments recruited geo-
graphically, and the number of battalions in each regiment
varied, just as did those of the British and French, in accordance with local circumstances. But the battalions were not
made up, preparatory to a military operation, into brigades
and divisions under such unit commanders as brigadiers and
divisional generals. It was the practice of the Russian commander in chief to dispose his battalions arbitrarily, in groups
but with no organized link between them, and equally arbitrarily he gave local command in each part of the field to one
or another of his subordinate generals. The system reflected
adherence to the principle of static warfare, as distinct from
tactical movement; there was no organization by which a large
portion of the available force could be maneuvered as one
unit. When, during the battle, Menshikov decided to move a
group of battalions across to another position, he led them off
personally, removing himself temporarily—and probably dis-
astrously—from over-all control of the battle.

Menshikov had some forty infantry battalions, with about
800 men each. Wherever they were placed, these battalions
were massed in columns of companies, each company comprising 200 men closely compacted in four ranks. The four
companies of a battalion moved equally closely in one solid
concentration, not with brisk military precision but with a
sort of ponderous deliberation—a dense mass of closely packed,
drab figures in long gray coats, whose forward movements
seemed less aggressive than irresistible. The soldiers kept their
position in close formation throughout the day and throughout the battle, standing or lying down, like herded cattle.

Eight battalions were posted in the vineyards on the south

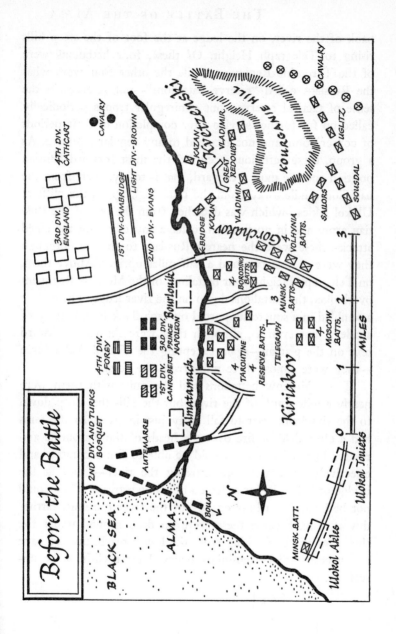

Before the Battle

bank of the river, on the ledge at the foot of the steep hills rising to Telegraph Height. Of these, four battalions were of the Taroutine Regiment, while the other four were what the Russians called "reserve battalions"—not reserves in the sense of tactical reserves, but semiregular troops periodically called up for further service after completion of their periods of conscription, and not attached to any regular regiment. As a group, these battalions occupied the most forward Russian position and the most westward; that is to say, apart from the battalion a mile away from the river high up on the cliffs at Ulukol Akles—which was detached from the rest of the Russian army and in no position to have any effect on the allied attack—these were the nearest Russians to the sea, although they were at least two and a half miles upriver. Above them, on Telegraph Height, four battalions of the Moscow Regiment overlooked the battalions down on the river ledge. These were assembled in a square supported on each flank by a battery of artillery, but even so, although they were the most leftward unit on the plateau—again excepting the Ulukol Akles force—they were almost three miles from the coast.

These Moscow battalions and the guns with them were nearly a mile south of the river, but the hills that drop down to the riverbank start to fall away just in front, so the guns had a clear field of fire over the heads of the Taroutine and reserve battalions. They would be able to fire accurately and effectively on any troops crossing the river—either at the bridge or below it, for at least a mile downstream. They could not be brought to bear on any of the river crossings farther downstream, because these were on dead ground under the shelter of the cliffs rising from the lower reach, but we have to remember that Menshikov believed these cliffs to be unscalable.

The road from the north crossed the river at the bridge and then entered a deep ravine, from which the ground rises steeply on each side and which itself rises steeply towards the south. The road climbed up the ravine in a sweeping curve to the west and reached the top of the plateau about two miles after it had crossed the river. Astride the road, on hillocks and ridges that look straight down onto the bridge, Menshikov placed four battalions of the Borodino Regiment, a battalion of riflemen, and two batteries of field artillery comprising sixteen guns in all. Behind these, higher up the hill and also astride the road, he kept what were really his only tactical reserves—four battalions of the Volhynia Regiment and three of the Minsk Regiment, and two more batteries of guns. In actual fact, these were placed so closely in the rear of the troops and guns covering the bridge that Menshikov in effect concentrated some twelve battalions of infantry and four batteries of guns on the road, as if he expected the allies to converge on the bridge and make their main attack up the ravine.

This left sixteen battalions of infantry disposed around Kourganie Hill—four each of the Kazan, Vladimir, Sousdal, and Uglitz Regiments. There were also two battalions made up of sailors drawn from the ships in Sebastopol harbor, but the Russians always looked on their sailors with disdain, mainly because they served in the navy voluntarily for long periods and no Russian could understand a man who chose to remain in a fighting service. Also, the narrow horizons of the Black and Baltic Seas hardly inspired the same spirit of maritime enterprise as did the wider seas sailed by the western Europeans, and the Russian sailor's lack of proper seagoing experience left him clumsy and unsure of himself, unable to elicit respect from his fellow countrymen.

Four of the sixteen infantry battalions were placed in two

long oblique lines right behind Kourganie Hill, where its
southerly slopes level out onto the plateau, at least two miles
from the river. The other twelve were grouped around Kourganie Hill itself, almost haphazardly. The most forward were
four Kazan battalions, two set in echelon on each side of the
Great Redoubt, on lines running at an angle from the ends of
the redoubt toward the river. Their combined effect was that
of a funnel, so that any enemy troops crossing the river and
climbing the little cliff that rose from the bank along the first
mile above the bridge would find their flanks assailed on each
side by these two battalions and would either be driven back
or compelled to advance straight toward the guns in the Great
Redoubt.

The other eight battalions were disposed around the
western end of the hill: four on the rising slopes directly behind the Great Redoubt, thereby covering it with considerable
strength; two behind the Lesser Redoubt; and two out of
sight behind the hill, whence they were to emerge at a critical
stage of the battle. The two battalions of sailors were posted
on their own, halfway between the hill and the lines of battalions in the rear on the edge of the plateau. Here they were
to remain throughout the battle, never called on to take any
active part.

Finally, the Russian right, that is to say the eastern slope
of Kourganie Hill, was covered by 3,400 cavalry—the Brigade
of Hussars and two regiments of Cossacks of the Don—with
three batteries of horse artillery.

The whole Russian force was arbitrarily divided into three
sectors merely for the purposes of command; Menshikov
placed his three major generals in command of the sectors.
General Kiriakov commanded the twelve battalions on the
left: the four Taroutine and the four reserve battalions on the

ledge beside the river, and the four Moscow battalions on Tele-graph Height—altogether a little more than 10,000 infantry. Prince Gorchakov commanded the twelve battalions astride the road—again about 10,000 infantry. General Kvetzenski commanded the sixteen battalions and the cavalry disposed around Kourganie Hill—about 13,000 infantry and 3,400 horse-men. Kiriakov had twenty guns on the left; Gorchakov had sixteen in the center, and Kvetzenski had some seventy in his sector, including the fourteen heavy guns from Sebastopol mounted in the Great Redoubt.

Kiriakov and Kvetzenski were undistinguished professional soldiers who had won their promotion by length of service. But Gorchakov was a member of a noble Russian family who had, characteristically, established his fame by suppressing a major insurrection in the Caucasus in 1820. Later he had been made governor of Eastern Siberia—an appointment which in those days was not regarded as a relegation. The governor of a province enjoyed the delegated despotism of the Tsar, and, although Nicholas liked to interfere wherever he could, Eastern Siberia was a long way from Moscow. Gorchakov had re-tired in 1851 with the rank of major general; at the outbreak of the Crimean War, he had voluntarily offered his services at the age of sixty-four and had been in command of the army of 60,000 men at Guirgevo, on the Danube, which had retreated to Bucharest as soon as it was attacked by the Turks. This failure was not altogether overlooked; faced with an enemy of very different caliber from the Turks, he had been relegated to a subordinate position as Menshikov's second-in-command, responsible for the center of the line.

The Russians had little respect for power at sea. Gorchakov probably shared the common Russian belief that, because they were primarily a maritime nation, the British knew little of war on land; their soldiers could therefore be classed in the same category as Russian sailors and were likely to be equally clumsy and ineffective. When the Russians saw British soldiers advancing toward them on the other side of the Alma River, their disdain was amply confirmed when the extended lines of infantry actually lay down on the ground. Compared with the French, who kept upright in their closely packed columns, the British were clearly about to prove themselves an insignificant enemy.

Even so, the combined force of the allies was more than the four reserve battalions down on the river ledge were willing to face. Menshikov had not shown particularly sound judgment when he placed his weakest troops in potentially the most dangerous position. When General Kiriakov came down to inspect their position—the most forward in the Russian line—he allowed himself some criticism of the commander in chief for their placement. (In truth, the wide ledge beside the stream was a strong defensive position which could command a long reach of the river; it was the only part of the front where Russian troops were actually waiting on the bank.) Showing some despondency even before the battle had started, Kiriakov doubted that, if these battalions were hard pressed, they would be able to withdraw up the steep slope of Telegraph Height; but he never actually sanctioned their removal; he could not have done so, in any case, without the consent of the commander in chief.

Nevertheless the general's expression of concern was enough for the reserves, and when Kiriakov left they started moving slowly back up the hill. The four Taroutine battalions, not relishing being left alone, followed—unobtrusively, step by step—until all eight had positioned themselves high up the face of Telegraph Height, almost at its crest, without the Russian generals being any the wiser.

6

WAITING FOR BOSQUET

O<small>F THE THREE ARMIES</small> drawn up on the banks of the Alma River, the French was best organized and equipped, mainly because of its recent action in Algeria. The chain of command was conventional enough—as was that of the British army—running downward from commander in chief, through divisions, brigades, and battalions, to companies.

The Russian army was quite different: it had no formal divisional or brigade structure, and, although the regiments were divided into battalions, these were grouped together quite arbitrarily; the commander of each battalion, which averaged 800 men, was responsible directly to the general commanding the whole formation. Without any intervening delegated command, these isolated units tended to act independently.

Each British and French infantry division was made up of two brigades. Each British brigade consisted of three battalions, and each battalion of 800 to 900 men. The French were not so consistent in the structure of their brigades, and their battalions were up to a thousand strong.

When making up the force to be sent out to Turkey, the

British authorities had drawn almost every battalion from a different regiment—probably so that the military honors to be won so easily might be shared as widely as possible. In the description of the battle that is to follow, each English battalion will be referred to by the name of the regiment of which it was a part: for instance, the only unit of the Welsh Regiment that went to the Crimea, at this stage of the war, was the 1st Battalion; to avoid confusion it will be referred to simply as the Welsh Regiment, or the Forty-first, to give it its official number. It was always the practice to name the battalions that made up any one formation—such as a brigade —in the order that they were placed from right to left along the line; this practice will be followed here.

The British and French infantry divisions that landed on the Crimea each had their own artillery batteries attached, and there was also a troop of horse artillery attached to the British cavalry. Although the Russians had a few 18-pound field guns, throwing an iron ball five inches in diameter, most of the allied guns were 9-pounders, throwing only a four-inch ball and with a range considerably less than 1,000 yards. The Russian field artillery consisted wholly of 18-pounders; and there were, of course, the 24- and 32-pound guns from the forts mounted in the Great Redoubt, which threw six- and six-and-a-half-inch balls—all with a range well in excess of 1,000 yards. The allied artillery was to suffer an even heavier handicap at the opening of the battle, because it was firing from a level below the Russians, who were up on the hill; in those days of comparatively weak propellants, the velocity of a projectile and, of course, the range were seriously reduced by a high trajectory. Only when, at a later stage, a couple of British guns were taken up to a position overlooking the Russians— and, on another occasion, when a French battery was able to surprise a Russian column at close quarters—were the allied guns to be of any real effect.

In small arms the allies were better off. The Minié rifle had first been introduced in France in 1848, and its use was already spreading through western Europe. The first weapon ever to have a rifled bore, it fired an oval bullet with an expanding cap in its base which engaged the rifling; the bullet and charge were still loaded through the muzzle and had to be rammed hard down the barrel. The Minié was fairly accurate, by the standards of those days, up to a range of 300 yards; it was actually sighted for 1,000 yards, but the velocity of the bullet at that range was something less than lethal. By the time the allies went to the Crimea, the French infantry was almost universally armed with the Minié rifle.

The British army, beset as it was by official inertia, had only just started to adopt the Minié, and these rifles had been issued to no more than a few selected marksmen in each regiment. Consequently most of the British infantrymen were still armed with the old smoothbore brown Bess musket. The only improvement that had been made to this musket since the Napoleonic wars had been the introduction of the percussion cap in place of the flintlock; but although the percussion cap was more certain in its action, and could be used in all weather, it took longer to set after each round than did the old method of priming the charge with a pinch of powder, and the rate of musket fire had been reduced from five to no more than three rounds a minute. The brown Bess certainly had a larger bore than the French and Russian muskets, but the advantage of this greater striking power at close range tended to be offset by the loss of velocity from which a heavier bullet inevitably suffered. It was unreliable in any circumstances, and ineffective at more than eighty yards, and the British were compelled to rely on numbers of muskets carried to close quarters rather than on marksmanship.

The Russian small arms were a long way behind even the British muskets. Half a century before, the great Russian general Suvorov had declared, "The bullet is a fool; the bayonet only is wise." It may have been wishful thinking, engendered by the inadequacy of Russian muskets, but Suvorov's maxim was still the credo of the Russian army at the beginning of the Crimean War—although after the Battle of the Alma it began to lose favor. So, although the allies were to face greatly superior artillery fire and were to suffer grievously from it, particularly at the start of the battle, the Russian muskets were not so effective until the combatants were at close quarters. (Of course, bullets fired promiscuously by even the most imperfect of muskets are dangerous, as the British were to find during their actual crossing of the river.)

The smoothbore muskets in both the Russian and British armies were still loaded with primitive cartridges consisting of a bullet and powder charge wrapped in paper. To load the gun, the paper had to be torn off—or, since only one hand was free, more conveniently bitten off. Then the loosened powder was poured into the barrel, and the bullet, still covered by the rest of the paper, was rammed home. It was a protracted process, especially in the heat of a battle. When Sir Colin Campbell had ordered the Highlanders "to get loose half their cartridges," these were not actually loaded into the muskets but would be ready when, as was certain to happen soon, the individual company commanders gave the order to load the first round.

At one o'clock, when Raglan and St. Arnaud parted after their inconclusive discussion, the British army marched forward again, still in its formation of grand divisions. In front were the Light Division on the left and the 2nd Division on the right, and behind these were the 1st and 3rd Divisions, so that the four divisions formed a square. There was, of course, a gap between the left-hand and right-hand divisions, because the whole concept of grand divisions was to allow room for each division to extend into line outwards from its center. In effect, these divisions were advancing in two parallel columns. Each column had a front of four companies—that is to say, sixteen files, with additional spaces between companies —which made it very much wider than the double company column of the French.

The incomplete 4th Division followed in the rear but over toward the left, out of line with the Light and 1st which it had followed on the previous day. Thus, although it was actually to the rear of the main square, it did in fact constitute a third parallel column, increasing the British army's over-all front by another sixteen files. This front therefore extended across three wide columns, presenting forty-eight files in all— the whole sufficiently spaced out so that it could be extended into line at any moment. (At least that was the intention, although the full spacing had been difficult to maintain.)

All morning, because the coastline as it ran south kept edging to the right, the British divisions had been harassed by repeated orders to incline equally to the right. As any man knows who has ever marched in a military formation—particularly one with a wide front—there is nothing more wearisome or irritating than to be assailed by continual nagging to ease to one flank or the other and, at the same time, keep the dressing and the correct space between the ranks. When the march was resumed at one o'clock, it appeared that during the morning the divisions had overdone their inclination to the right; they were too near the French, and insufficient room had been left for extending into line. Consequently the whole process had to be repeated, this time easing the files back to the left.

Around the open extremities of the British army—to the front, on the left, and to the rear—a thin line of riflemen was extended in skirmishing order. Beyond these, half a dozen squadrons of cavalry were spaced out—about 500 horsemen in all, who could hardly have put up much effective resistance to a determined attack by Menshikov's 3,400 cavalrymen waiting on the other side of river.

Soon after one o'clock, the skirmishers came within range of their opposite numbers, who were lying in front of the foremost Russian battalions in the vineyards just below the bridge, and the Battle of the Alma was opened by a single Russian musket shot which kicked up a little spurt of dust, behind the line of British skirmishers but just in front of the foremost files of the advancing Light Division. Within a few seconds, a Russian field gun on the slopes of Kourganie Hill opened fire, and round shot started falling on the north bank of the river, still ahead of the advancing British soldiers. It was clear that the time had come to deploy the leading divisions into line, and the whole army was halted for this purpose.

The deployment of 10,000 men from column into line is an evolution of some magnitude. Each separate company had practiced it on the parade ground times without number; unfortunately, here, despite all the nagging by regimental and noncommissioned officers, the Light Division had not edged far enough to the left, and there was insufficient room for the 2nd Division to extend into line without overlapping the Light. A division in line—two ranks of 2,500 men each—would

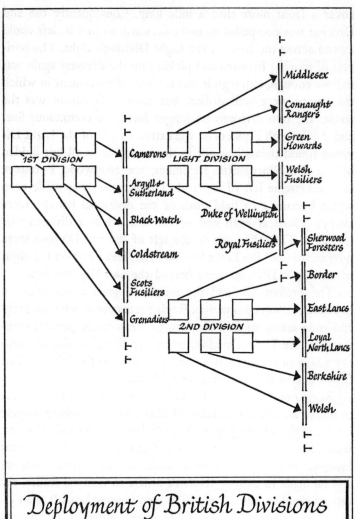

Deployment of British Divisions into Line (NOT TO SCALE)

cover a front more than a mile long. Consequently the 2nd Division was compelled to move forward, so that its left could extend across the front of the Light Division's right. The business of moving forward and picking up the dressing again was tedious enough, although it was the sort of movement in which the troops were well drilled, but more unfortunate was the result: the two divisions no longer formed a continuous line, and the Seventh Fusiliers on the extreme right of the Light Division found themselves not in the front line at all but hidden behind the Ninety-fifth Regiment, the Sherwood Foresters, on the extreme left of the 2nd. The situation was made even worse because two field guns of the divisional battery were always placed at each end of the line when a division was extended. Thus the guns on the left of the 2nd Division were now in front of the Light Division line, and those on the right of the Light Division were behind the 2nd Division line.

The broken line and the misplaced guns could create a hopelessly involved situation. Raglan recognized it immediately and rode across to find Sir George Brown, the general commanding the Light Division, intending to order him to move the whole of his division, as one unit, over to the left and then forward into line with the 2nd Division.

Raglan could not find Sir George immediately, so he spoke to one of his brigadiers, General Codrington, of whose brigade on the right of the Light Division line the Seventh Fusiliers were part. Codrington recognized that the proposed movement involved not only his own brigade but the whole division, and he made to convey Raglan's orders to General Buller, the other brigadier. But, as we have seen before, Lord Raglan always avoided unpleasantness. On second thought, he realized that a movement of the division that was not by order of the divisional general might cause that general to be remarkably unpleasant, so he recalled Codrington and rescinded the order.

Sir George Brown, the general in question, was known as one of the most churlish officers in the army. He was older than Raglan and had fought at Corunna even before Raglan had gone out to the Peninsula as Wellington's aide-de-camp. He hated interference; only the year before he had made an ostentatious retirement from the army in objection to some minor reforms that were being introduced. When war was declared he had come back, because he was sure the army could not manage without him; although he was over seventy, he had assumed he would at least be given command of a division, as, in fact, had happened.

This is not to suggest that Raglan was intimidated by Sir George Brown; Raglan was intimidated by no one. Nor was he always punctilious in respecting the chain of command when dealing with subordinates. Only recently, when the army was at Varna, he had caused considerable resentment by entirely disregarding Lord Lucan, the general commanding the cavalry division, to deal directly with Lord Cardigan, the brigadier of the cavalry's Light Brigade, who was Lucan's subordinate—and, incidentally, his brother-in-law and implacable personal enemy. But now, although a direct order to the brigadier might have removed a latent cause of calamity, Raglan decided that it might embarrass Sir George Brown if he interfered.

That Sir George never took the initiative to move his division over to the left was mainly because of his poor sight; it had deteriorated as he aged, but he obstinately refused to wear glasses. He had happened to ride off toward the left of the line and could not see what was going on from even a short distance. Any other general would at least have carried some form of field glass, or even a telescope, but Sir George dismissed the need for such an affectation. By the time he did realize what had happened, the lines were moving forward again and it was too late to remedy the situation.

So far, only the two leading divisions had extended into line; the others were still following in open column of companies. Soon, the two rear divisions, the 1st and 3rd, also found themselves under fire. This time Raglan was taking no risk that they might not have enough room to deploy; he ordered the commander of the 1st, the Duke of Cambridge, to extend his division into line, but he held back the 3rd Division, ordering it to remain in column and take its place alongside the incomplete 4th Division and behind the extended 1st. The British army was now drawn up in two lines of two ranks each—the front line, consisting of two divisions, broken in the center so that one of its halves overlapped the other, and the rear line, of one division only—with two more divisions in column behind them. Each of the two ranks in each divisional line stretched for more than a mile, and so the long ranks of British soldiers standing shoulder to shoulder ran for at least six miles in all.

By now the extended lines were coming under considerable fire from the Russian skirmishers in the vineyards and from the guns on the hill, and Raglan must have begun to regret that he had failed to agree on a concerted plan with St. Arnaud. He could see Bosquet's division moving down toward the river on the right, presumably following St. Arnaud's plan to cross at the mouth and climb the cliffs, in an attempt to turn the Russian left. But he had no idea what the rest of the French army intended to do, although the relative positions in which the two armies were approaching the river virtually determined the tactics.

In addition to Almatamack, there was another small village

on the north bank, called Bourlouik, about a quarter of a mile below the bridge. It lay huddled against the river directly opposite the wide ledge on the other side on which the forward Russian battalions were waiting in the vineyards. The extreme right of the British army was in line with Bourlouik village—although the village was still nearly a mile away—and even though the French were not extended into line but were still advancing in their long, snakelike columns, it was clear that the front on which they would operate would have to be between Bourlouik and the mouth of the river. (A little later that afternoon, just as the British army was to start its final move down to the river, the Russians set fire to Bourlouik because it was offering useful cover to the advancing troops. The smoke and the flames forced the right extremity of the British line to divide and pass on each side of the village. But just now, Bourlouik seemed to mark the right of the British front.)

The British lines were still a mile away from the river, and it was evident to Raglan that he must hold back his own troops until the French crossed and attacked on their front, after which his assault could be launched while the attention of the Russians was being diverted. The sequence must be: first, Bosquet's right hook; then, the main French assault on the leftward Russian positions; and, finally, the British attack straight across the river. To repeat, this was no preconceived plan, agreed on by the allied generals; it was merely the way Raglan now expected the battle to develop.

The British lines were coming within range of the Russian guns when Raglan decided to halt, and the first casualties were taking place. Since few of the rank and file had been in action before, the first lesson of war they learned was how death could strike with stealth and unexpectedness.

At first it seemed so simple to avoid being hit. When a man saw a puff of smoke from one of the big guns high up on the hill, he could watch the round shot in its trajectory quite easily, guess where it was going to fall—and usually it fell in some other part of the field. Round shot was not too dangerous when fired at a gun's maximum range with a high plunging trajectory, because, although a ball from one of the heavier Russian guns could carry up to some 1,200 yards, unless it made a very lucky direct hit it usually buried itself in the ground. Fired short, however, at a low trajectory, the ball would ricochet along the ground and could still be lethal a mile away. The gunners in the Crimean War were to become quite skilled in the use of the ricochet, even, during the siege of Sebastopol, using it laterally to deflect shots round corners.

If a shot did strike the ground ahead and start bounding directly toward a soldier, he still had time, if he was quick about it, to open ranks by stepping backwards and behind the next man and let the shot pass through his rank harmlessly. Not that stepping out of line was encouraged; but it was worth the rebuke of a sergeant to avoid decapitation by a cannon ball. Most of the heavy guns fired plain round shot, which was only lethal if it made a direct hit. Some fired grapeshot, also known as canister—thin metal cylinders stuffed with loose metal, or even stones—that burst on impact into a dangerous shower of missiles, although their effective range was much shorter. Artillery barrels were not yet rifled, and only the smaller field guns fired what were known as shells— hollow iron spheres stuffed with gunpowder and ignited with a fuse. (That is how the shell got its name: it was simply a hollow shell of metal.) By a crude timing device, the length of fuse could be altered, and skillful gunners could make these shells burst just above the heads of the troops they were firing at, so that they had the effect of shrapnel.

The soldiers discovered that death, when it came, came usually without warning; the first casualty in the British army that day was an artillery driver who simply fell forward, off his horse, before any of his comrades realized that a shot of any sort had come along. Soon, silent unheralded death was striking indiscriminately along the lines, and the illusion that this war was going to be easy was once and for all dispelled.

The army was halted: the men in the long lines of the 2nd, the Light, and the 1st Divisions were ordered to lie down, while the 3rd and 4th Divisions, still out of range of enemy fire, stood waiting behind in their columns. For the men on the ground, an ordeal followed that was to last for nearly an hour and a half. Fifteen thousand men lay shoulder to shoulder within range of the Russian guns, on ground that sloped down toward the river, each prone British soldier presenting an almost full-length target to the gunners on the heights. The shorter-range British guns were unable to reply, but even the smaller field guns of the Russians were beginning to take advantage of their elevated positions. The bursting of the little shells—while almost harmless compared to the high explosive shells we know today—made a spray of nasty, penetrating splinters which caused painful head and flesh wounds and frequently found some more vulnerable spot.

It is quite an ordeal to lie down on an open slope to be fired upon; even the hardest battle-trained troops would not relish it. For the first time in forty years, the discipline of the British army was put to the test. The gallant spirit that resulted (and was evinced time and time again in the Crimean War) was something more than the result of harsh discipline. Each man behaved according to character. Some faced the ordeal unconcernedly; others, feeling less brave, covered their fear with a veneer of nervous humor, to conceal it from their neighbors in the ranks. It was a relief to crack insipid little jokes: to give girls' names to each of the guns up on the hill, report when Josephine or Emmeline had fired, and predict with exaggerated ribaldry where her shot would land; to call out to the officers riding past, respectfully warning them of the imminent approach of a round shot but, even so, giving the warning a bawdy twist. Then a soldier might hear a muffled cry beside him, or a horrible scream, and feel his neighbor struggling convulsively, his hot blood spurting. The men on either side might rise cautiously to their knees and drag the injured man clumsily out of the way, forward or backward from the ranks, to writhe in agony, untended; for to move a stricken man was to disobey orders. Sir Colin Campbell rode up and down the lines of the Highland regiments in the 1st Division, telling them, "Whoever is wounded must lie where he is until a bandsman comes to attend to him—I don't care what his rank is. No soldiers must go carrying off wounded men. If any soldier does such a thing, his name shall be stuck up in his parish church." So a man could not escape from the ordeal by pretending he was braving the enemy fire to carry a wounded comrade out of danger.

While the rank and file lay in lines, targets for the enemy guns, the mounted senior officers invited the gunners' fire even more challengingly, although for the most part they kept moving. Brigadiers and divisional generals each rode, with their attendants, up and down their own lines—General Codrington's white Arab pony made him particularly conspicuous —and Lord Raglan himself, with his staff, moved or stood in discussion within range of the enemy shot, quite unconcerned. The British officers in the Crimean War, from commander

in chief down, may have committed dreadful—in many instances, unforgivable—tactical blunders; they enjoyed a relative luxury in their quarters that bears no comparison with
the privations suffered by the rank and file; yet in the actual
campaigning—in the waiting, the fighting, the suffering from
wounds, the dying—they showed as much unflinching bravery
as the men in the ranks and very often stood out in front to
take the brunt of the enemy attack. It is often said that the
British soldiers in the Crimean War made up by their personal
bravery for the dreadful mistakes of their leaders; but having
made their mistakes, the leaders always stood by the soldiers
and just as gallantly retrieved the blunders they themselves
had made.

Raglan could be seen clearly enough by the Russians
through their telescopes, in his blue frock coat with its empty
sleeve, and white-plumed, cocked hat. In fact, unlike the
modern practice of making commanding officers as inconspicuous as possible, the British commander in chief and his
staff purposely advertised themselves, and the Russians could
have had little difficulty in distinguishing them. Not that the
shooting was so accurate that even a group of horsemen could
be picked off at the extreme range at which the Russian guns
were firing. But all the same, Raglan and his staff were un-
mistakably under fire, and as a group they were more likely
to be hit by round shot than the prone figures in the ranks,
over whom many of the shots ricocheted quite harmlessly. In
fact, the whole purpose of making the troops lie down was so
that they would present a less vulnerable target. Raglan was
intent on setting his men an example of absolute calm, and
when he sent an aide-de-camp with an order to one of the
divisional generals, he particularly told him, "Go quietly; don't
gallop!" There can be no doubt that Raglan's bearing, which

he communicated to his staff, had much to do with the steadiness with which the British lines waited that afternoon by the Alma.

Although the French 2nd Division under General Bosquet never actually became engaged with the Russians during the battle except by the exchange of some artillery fire, the way in which it made the first crossing of the river and climbed up onto the plateau on top of the cliffs was in itself something of an achievement. At one o'clock Bosquet and his staff rode down toward the riverbank. In addition to noting the sand bar at the river mouth, they saw that the ford at Almatamack led to a narrow road on the other side of the river. This road wound up a ravine cutting through the sheer face of the cliffs and appeared good enough to take guns, although in parts it seemed cut by deep ruts, and the broken ground rising from each side suggested possible ambush.

The report from the ships had told Bosquet about the path up the cliff face from the shore, and here was a second way up to the plateau. The sailors had said that they could see no Russians on the plateau except those way back at Ulukol Akles. But it was difficult for anyone on the ships to be certain that there were no enemy positions along the cliffs rising from the riverbank, and the sailors had certainly not noticed the ravine opposite Almatamack in which an enemy force might well have been placed. Bosquet had to decide from his own observation whether or not he was likely to meet any opposition; for to climb to the top of the plateau his men would have to march up the road in column, and even the lightest Russian force would be able to stop them and inflict heavy damage.

Bosquet, at forty-five, was a comparatively young general. He had served in Algeria for ten years, where he had had plenty of experience in moving troops up steep hills and through narrow passes. While the campaigns against the Arab tribes had not demanded a high degree of military ability, they had given him ample practice in operating in difficult country. He was a characteristic, volatile Frenchman, alive with energy and enterprise, in marked contrast to the other divisional generals with the French army in the field that day, and he was probably more qualified than any of the other generals, British or French, to command the troops who were to cross the river near its mouth and find their way up the cliffs and onto the plateau.

Bosquet's division comprised two brigades of 3,000 infantrymen each, and twelve guns; and he also had the 9,000 Turks under his command. His brigadiers were Generals Bouat and Autemarre. He attached the Turks to Bouat's brigade, giving him 12,000 men in all—in the circumstances, a tremendous force, whose strength was to be entirely wasted—and sent him to cross the river by the sand bar at its mouth. He inclined Autemarre's brigade to the left, toward Almatamack. When the two brigades started to move forward again at half-past one, they each took six guns, but it soon became evident that no artillery could be taken across the sand bar or dragged up the narrow cliff path, so Bouat's batteries were detached and given to Autemarre. Before either of the brigades moved off, the French soldiers were ordered to take off their packs, which carried their rations, eating utensils, and spare clothing, and lay them on the ground; thus were they committed to battle. (A little later, two more French divisions—12,000 more men—were to do the same, so that some 18,000 French packs would litter the ground that sloped down to the river.)

Bosquet himself rode down to the ford at Almatamack and joined Autemarre at the head of his brigade. It was ten minutes past two when their two horses splashed across the shallow ford at the head of 3,000 men, still in column, with the guns interposed at intervals along its length. Bosquet seemed confident that there would be no ambush along the road and rode boldly up to the top, with the battalions tramping behind him. To Bosquet and his brigadier it was a familiar enough situation, and they did nothing to discourage some of the Zouave infantrymen from breaking away quite spontaneously from the winding line of march and climbing the steep face of the ravine to make their way onto the plateau as fast as they could. As volunteer regiments, the Zouaves approached the prospect of battle with an enthusiasm quite foreign to the ordinary French conscript. The sailors on the ships lying off the mouth of the river watched with admiration as they swarmed up cliffs that other infantrymen would have deliberately avoided.

When Bosquet came out onto the plateau, the nearest enemy formations he could see were General Kiriakov's battalions on Telegraph Height at least a mile and a half away. None of Bouat's men had yet emerged on the top of the cliffs; in fact, the passage over the sand bar was proving a protracted exercise because, although the sea was calm and the surf relatively light, the waves that did break over the bar were insistent enough to make the soldiers brace themselves to keep their footholds, so that the crossing had to be made slowly, each man shuffling along through the water. To add to the delay, when they found the path up the cliff it was so narrow and winding that it took the first files nearly half an hour to struggle up it. (Bosquet's 12,000 men were to spend so much time crossing the river and climbing up to the plateau that when they all reached the top the Battle of the Alma was virtually over.)

Despite his enterprise in hurrying Autemarre's brigade

forward up the road from Almatamack, Bosquet seemed unable to decide what next to do now that he was on the plateau. No doubt, if he had found himself immediately face to face with the enemy, he would have taken positive action. In the distance, the Russian formations at the top of Telegraph Height could be seen to be moving; and General Kiriakov was bringing two battalions of the Moscow Regiment in Bosquet's direction, but these two battalions separated and took up new static positions more than a mile away, one high up on the plateau and the other lower down. Naturally Bosquet had to wait for his whole column to emerge from the ravine—and for the guns—before he could make any further move. Not surprisingly, one of the wheels of his leading gun fell into a deep rut in the road, and there followed a considerable delay before the way was cleared and any of the guns were able to reach the top.

By now the Russians at Ulukol Akles had seen the first Zouaves climb onto the plateau; they had hurriedly moved four of their own guns to Ulukol Touiets, another little hamlet about a quarter of a mile inland, whence they were within range of the road where it debouched onto the ravine. There is no doubt that the Russians units were waiting for an attack that day, so the appearance of the first Zouaves did not take them altogether by surprise and the guns at Ulukol Touiets opened fire quickly enough. When the round shot started falling, the Zouaves had no option but to drop back down into the ravine and take cover behind the banks at the top.

In a comparatively short time the road was cleared, and the French guns were brought up onto the plateau to answer the Russian fire. Although Bosquet had still not decided to move forward, he drew up his brigade behind the guns—which were now exchanging shots with the Russians—and waited for something to develop. The Russian fire was disconcerting enough for those few who found themselves in the path of the shots coming over, but, harassed by the French guns that were now replying, it had a negligible effect on the full brigade.

7

THE HESITANT
DIVISIONS

T HE STORY IS TOLD that, when Marshal St. Arnaud gathered
his generals together before ordering the advance of the French
army, he declared theatrically, "With such men as you, I
have no orders to give! I have but to point to the enemy!"
This was one way to avoid making any tactical decisions himself; beyond the superficial plan that he had proposed to
Raglan, he had given no thought as to how the battle should
be conducted.

It was clear that covering the whole battlefront with the
French army while sending the British around the Russian
flank, as he had urged so forcefully the night before, was not
feasible. Now that the Russian front could be seen to stretch
for more than five miles inland, it was just as well that Raglan
had so arbitrarily disregarded his proposals. In any case, it
would have been quite out of character for the French to extend their divisions into line in the way he had suggested. He
had every reason to be glad that he had only to point to the
enemy; he would not now have to prevail on his generals to
depart from their invariable practice of operating in column.

However, the least that could be expected of a commander in chief would be to give some thought to the individual moves that his divisions were to make, if only from the aspect of how they would act in relation to each other. In his plan proposed the night before, St. Arnaud had given no indication of where any units except Bosquet's division might be expected to cross the river, because he had no knowledge of where river crossings might be possible, other than over the sand bar that had been reported to him by the fleet. But now he and his generals were able to scan the river and its banks through their telescopes, and when Bosquet reported the ford at Almatamack, St. Arnaud agreed that one of his brigades should make a crossing there.

A mile farther upriver, a white farmhouse stood in the corner of one of the vineyards on the north bank: a distinctive landmark. A second ravine could be seen cut into the cliffs immediately opposite the farmhouse, with what looked like a fair road running up it, although the climb was as steep as that from Almatamack. It was reasonable to suppose that the river was fordable at this point; otherwise the road would have no purpose. About three quarters of a mile farther upriver, halfway between the white house and Bourlouik village, where the cliffs gave way to more easily scalable slopes, another ford was clearly discernible, and from this ford a road rose up toward Telegraph Height in a more gradual ascent. In fact, three or four tracks could be seen climbing the slopes almost opposite, but slightly below, Bourlouik; since Raglan had deftly appropriated to the British army the whole front above the village, on the sector where the slopes were relatively gentle, these tracks offered the French their most straightforward access to the Russian positions.

The role of Bosquet's 2nd Division had been decided the

night before, although the plan for turning the Russian left had now been amended to include the approach from Alma-tamack. St. Arnaud directed the French 1st Division, under General Canrobert, to cross at the white farmhouse, and the 3rd Division, under General Prince Napoleon, to cross at the ford below Bourlouik. The 4th Division under General Forey was held in reserve. Thus the intention was to funnel about 24,000 men (including the Turks) with their divisional batteries, a total of forty-eight guns, into four narrow river crossings—at the sand bar, opposite Almatamack, at the white farmhouse, and across the ford below Bourlouik—and all these troops were to debouch in closely packed columns onto the enemy-held south bank. Less than half these men were actually to cross to the other side of the river, but that does not alter the fact that St. Arnaud proposed that they should.

The whole conception of the French assault differed from that of the British, who were covering their front with one extended line and who apparently intended to cross the river in that formation. The French commanders might well have argued that the only possible way to cross was to use the established fords and that the British army was inviting disaster by believing that the men would be able to wade through the river at any point they approached; no one had any knowledge of the river's depth. But the problem never really presented itself to St. Arnaud, because the French army traditionally made its moves in column. Having decided on the places at which each division was to cross, the Marshal believed he had no more to do than point to the enemy and leave the next moves to his generals.

In the abilities of these generals, it might be more difficult to find much justification for St. Arnaud's confidence—except, perhaps, in the case of Bosquet. All four were comparatively young men. Bosquet was only forty-five, as was Canrobert, the commander of the 1st Division. Like Bosquet, Canrobert had spent nearly ten years in Algeria. He now held the Emperor's "dormant commission," which meant that if anything happened to St. Arnaud he would succeed to command in the field (this occurred, in fact, within a few days). Canrobert had distinguished himself as a professional soldier and had acquired a deserved reputation for bravery in action. But perhaps the sort of courage needed to fight Arabs in the mountains and deserts of Algeria, sterling as it must have been, is something different from the courage needed to grapple with the persistent cares of a high-ranking commander. When the armies suffered from the cholera epidemic in Bulgaria, he showed a lack of that fortitude which would have enabled him to contend with the disaster. (The time was to come, after he succeeded to command in the Crimea, when he would find the responsibilities an intolerable burden. In the end he was reduced to pleading with one of his subordinate generals to take over the command.)

Bosquet, of the 2nd Division, we have already described. The 3rd Division was commanded by Prince Jerome Napoleon, first cousin of the Emperor and, like him, a nephew of Napoleon I. He was a soldier by profession but had given scant attention to military affairs, and he had seen no active service of any sort—an unusual situation in the French army of that period, made possible only because of his family connections. After the Crimean War, the world came to know him as Plon Plon—a distortion of the French phrase *plomb plomb*, signifying a fear of lead bullets. The allegation that he suffered from this fear had its birth at the Battle of the Alma, although he was not given the opportunity actually to test his personal courage in this battle. At thirty-two, he was absurdly young and inexperienced to be a divisional general.

The general commanding the 4th Division, General Forey, was a veteran at fifty. Like the other generals—except Prince Napoleon—he had seen active service in Algeria. But he was to take no active part in the Battle of the Alma, because St. Arnaud finally ordered the two brigades of his division to move forward separately—one to support Bosquet and one to Prince Napoleon—so that Forey himself was left with no troops to command.

The British army was still halted as Bosquet emerged onto the plateau. For more than an hour the British lines had been suffering a punishing fire from the Russian guns. At the time the Russians opened fire, the French 1st and 3rd Divisions had been waiting in their columns at about the same distance from the river as the British lines, but they received no enemy fire at first, because the conformation of the cliffs shielded them from the positions in which the Russian guns had been placed. When word came to General Kiriakov that the enemy had crossed the river at Almatamack and were climbing the road up to the plateau, he detached two battalions of the Moscow Regiment from their positions on Telegraph Height and moved them over toward the west—one still remaining on the plateau, the other placed a little way down the slope toward the river— and with each of these battalions he had sent a battery of guns. The move had really been made to counter Bosquet's advance, but Bosquet's men were still out of practical range; the gunners, now they could look down over the crest of the cliffs, saw that Canrobert's and Prince Napoleon's divisions, halted in solid columns before them, presented much more inviting targets. So the round shot came bounding toward the French forma- tions, and the French soldiers standing massed together offered even more sacrificial targets to the enemy than had the prone British lines.

It was now nearly half-past two; the time had come for the second phase of this battle which seemed, at any rate for the time being, to be following a rational sequence despite the lack of an over-all plan. The next move was for Canrobert to lead his column down to the white farmhouse. Preceded by a screen of skirmishers—who, in the accepted practice of the French army, fired their rifles promiscuously as they advanced, whether they could see the enemy ahead or not—the 1st Division moved forward. Because the river was shallow and readily fordable—although no actual causeway had been constructed —the column crossed with no difficulty other than that caused by the enemy's gunfire, although the effect of this was reduced as the troops in the van of the column came under cover of the high cliffs. The road up the ravine turned out to be comparatively smooth and easy but too narrow for any guns. For the time being, Canrobert left his batteries down on the river ledge, which at this point was some 500 yards wide; but when it was reported to him that Bosquet had been able to take his guns onto the plateau, he ordered his own batteries back across the river and down to Almatamack so that they could climb the road Bosquet had taken and make their way along the crest of the cliffs to rejoin him at the top.

Meanwhile, he decided that until he had his guns he could not make any advance onto the plateau. There was a strong belief in the French army—so strong that it had come to be accepted by some commanders almost as an axiom—that infantry could not operate in any circumstances without artillery support; as a result, infantry formations were in danger of losing their self-reliance. It was as if every soldier believed that he ought to be armed with a field gun because without one he was incapable of fighting.

Having decided that it would be dangerous for his 5,000 men to emerge onto the plateau, Canrobert extended the eight battalions forming his division, each in its own battalion column, on the sides of the road down in the comfortable protection of the ravine. As soon as the whole division crossed the river, it was protected from Kiriakov's guns by the hills rising before it, and Canrobert sat down to wait for his own guns to make their way around by Almatamack, which might take up to half an hour.

Prince Napoleon was even less enterprising. He led the 3rd Division in eight battalion columns down the slope toward the ford below Bourlouik. This move carried the division to its left, higher up the river, so that the steepest part of the cliffs no longer screened it from the Russian guns. Consequently Prince Napoleon's men found themselves under heavy fire, from the main Russian batteries on Telegraph Height as well as from the two batteries which Kiriakov had moved.

Overcome by this gunfire, the French battalions broke away from their brigade formation, each one seeking cover where it could in the vineyards and gardens, still on the north bank; the 3rd Division's brave advance was halted before it even reached the river. When it had first moved forward, St. Arnaud and his headquarters staff had placed themselves in the middle of the divisional column. When the column broke up into separate battalions they found themselves left in an isolated little group in one of the gardens by the river. There they simply awaited developments. What the French army would do or not do was now quite beyond the Marshal's control.

Prince Menshikov had established his headquarters on Kourganie Hill, convinced that the only part of the river that the enemy would attempt to cross would be either at or above the road bridge. When word came to him at about one o'clock that a large force—which, in actual fact, was 12,000 strong —was making its way down the north bank toward the river mouth, he refused to believe that the report had any significance. He was certain there was no access to the plateau west of the bridge except up the steep slopes of Telegraph Height, where at least a dozen of his infantry battalions were waiting. West of these men, the Russian line was amply protected by steep cliffs.

Menshikov was a bully by nature, and he would listen to no one who disagreed with him. He angrily dismissed a suggestion by one of his staff that there might be some possibility of this large force finding its way onto the plateau to threaten the Russian left; like all bullies, he became even more angry when it was at last reported to him that Bosquet's soldiers had already appeared on the plateau.

With the typical reaction of the autocrat unwilling to delegate authority, Menshikov ordered an emergency force to be detached from the formations waiting on the heights and, without telling any of his generals, hurried away to the west himself, leaving the rest of the Russian army to face the most critical sector of the front without an over-all command. He took two batteries of guns, the three battalions of the Minsk Regiment from the main reserve near the road, and all four battalions of the Moscow Regiment from Telegraph Height, including the two that General Kiriakov had just moved towards the west. Sending messages to these units ordering them to follow him, he rode off with a squadron of Hussars, straight across country towards Ulukol Touiets, at least five miles from Kourganie Hill.

When Menshikov reached Ulukol Touiets, some twenty minutes after Bosquet's men had first appeared on the plateau, he had to wait some time before the first of his additional guns arrived after their long haul. But the activity at Ulukol Touiets, when Menshikov arrived with his staff, was noticed by the fleet and the ships' guns opened fire. Either by superb gunnery on the part of the sailors, or more likely by pure chance, four of the staff were hit within a few minutes—a calamity that seemed to convince Menshikov that the western part of the plateau was unhealthy. As soon as the infantry battalions, forced-marched across the plateau, started to arrive at Ulukol Toiuets, he turned them about and sent them back to their former positions with orders to lose no time. It was the sort of situation to which the Tsar's soldiers were well used, and most of them were probably only too thankful that this abortive maneuver kept them away so long from the fighting. The whole exercise occupied Menshikov for over an hour; by the time he and the troops that he had drawn off returned to the center of the line, the battle proper was joined and, although much was yet to happen, the outcome was already virtually decided.

8

"THE INFANTRY WILL ADVANCE"

By HALF-PAST TWO a lull came over the field. Apart from exchanges of artillery fire, the French had made no contact with the enemy; and the men of the three leading British divisions were still lying face down. There had been a lively engagement, on the extreme left of the British front, between riflemen of the 2nd Battalion of the Rifle Brigade, led by Major Norcutt, and Russian skirmishers lodged in the vineyards on the north bank. The riflemen, in skirmishing order themselves, had moved down to the walls skirting the vineyards. They exchanged fire with the Russians at close range and drove them over to the other bank. It was a minor engagement, but it did at least mark an opening of the actual fighting.

Once this little skirmish was over, all activity on the battlefield seemed to cease. Menshikov was making his impulsive dash to the west, but his line of march was more than a mile from the river and the movement could not be seen from anywhere down in the valley. The only disturbance to the peace came from the Russian guns, of which at least thirty were firing steadily at the British lines and French columns. Soldiers were still being struck down at random by round shot and shrapnel, left to endure their wounds where they fell if they were not killed outright. Otherwise there was no sign of movement, except from little groups of horsemen moving quietly up and down the British lines.

Shortly after half-past two, Lord Raglan and his staff rode along the front of the 2nd Division, almost at the extreme right of the British line. Raglan stopped to determine, through his telescope, what the French were doing. It was clear that they were making no further move forward and that St. Arnaud's plan to open the battle by assaulting the Russian left had not materialized. The British soldiers' ordeal of lying on the ground under continual fire was weighing heavily on their commander. He was supremely brave himself, but he could not fail to be affected by the losses his troops were suffering and by the frustration that every man in the army must have been feeling.

As long as the preliminaries to the battle followed a certain tactical pattern, Raglan had been loath to order the British army to move forward until this advance could fall into its logical place. But now it seemed that the Russians were not being engaged on their left after all. Raglan saw nothing of Menshikov's sudden stampede to the west; for all he knew, the Russians were still untroubled by the French, because it was clear enough to anyone down by the river that the French 1st and 3rd Divisions were both holding back—a circumstance which in itself might indicate that Bosquet had not yet engaged the enemy.

So, as far as Raglan could tell, the whole Russian force on the heights—of whose strength he was still quite ignorant—was available to oppose a British attack. Moreover, there was always the possibility that, as soon as the British advanced, the Russians might seize the tactical initiative themselves, set upon

Canrobert's and Prince Napoleon's highly vulnerable divisions, and drive them back. Then their way would be clear to swing around the right flank of the British army just as it was engaged in the absorbing process of crossing the river. So far, the behavior of the French divisions had done little to suggest that they would be able to withstand much enemy pressure. Of course, there was also the possibility that the Russian cavalry, massed on the slopes of Kourganie Hill, might ride around the other flank to attack the British left and complete the pincer effect, but that hazard would remain even were the battle to follow the pattern Raglan had expected. Raglan was overwhelmingly impatient to get his soldiers off the ground and moving forward, but at the same time he was well aware that a British advance launched while the French divisions remained in their present situations had its dangers.

While Raglan sat quietly on his horse, a little detached from the rest of his staff—for he was an aloof man and not given to taking subordinates into his confidence—a young French aide-de-camp came cantering toward him. It is not clear whether this young man came from St. Arnaud; or whether Bosquet had sent him directly to Raglan; or even whether Bosquet had originally sent him to St. Arnaud, who had sent him on to Raglan. But he was in an agitated state as he told Raglan in French that unless something could be done immediately Bosquet would be "compromised."

Raglan spoke French almost as well as he spoke English, and equally carefully. He happened to have a particular distaste for the French verb *compromettre*, in a military context. He never used the word; it seemed to him obscure and almost meaningless. Speaking quietly to the aide-de-camp—for he seldom showed impatience—he asked the young Frenchman what would happen if Bosquet were "compromised." The young officer answered despairingly, *"Il battra en retraite"* (He will beat a retreat).

It is doubtful if this message to Raglan had any authoritative origin. Although Bosquet was not taking any initiative on the plateau, he was being assailed by nothing worse than a few long-range artillery shots to which his own guns were replying with some effect. Nor was Bosquet a general without plenty of self-reliance. (In that, he differed considerably from Canrobert and Prince Napoleon, both of whom had already displayed an inability to depend on their own resources when faced, for the first time in their careers, with an imposing enemy.) Nevertheless, it is possible that St. Arnaud—enveloped in Prince Napoleon's column, which was now at a complete halt, apparently held up by some fearful obstacle—was disturbed because he could see that Bosquet's advance onto the plateau was not being followed up by the French 1st and 3rd Divisions. St. Arnaud might well have believed that if Bosquet was given no support he would find himself in a compromising position; the wording of the message was probably St. Arnaud's own, intended to imply that Bosquet was not being supported in the manner that he had been given to expect.

Whatever its origin or meaning, and however false a picture it suggested of Bosquet's position, the message had the effect of making up Raglan's mind. He turned to General Airey, the Quartermaster General, and said, "The infantry will advance." This was the last executive order he gave during the battle, but, although it was based on no tactical reasoning, it was a courageous decision under the circumstances. The British army was now committed.

The order was transmitted to the divisional generals by one of Raglan's own aides-de-camp, a dashing young cavalry officer named Captain Nolan. (It was Captain Nolan, on a historic occasion a few weeks later, who galloped impetuously down a steep escarpment into the Balaklava valley to transmit the order from Raglan that sent the Light Brigade of cavalry on its epic charge against the Russian guns. History suggests that, on that occasion, it was not Raglan's intention that the charge should be made in the direction it took but that Nolan distorted Raglan's words and thereby caused the tragic blunder. Nolan joined in the charge but was killed almost immediately.)

This time, because Raglan had given express instructions to the staff to behave calmly, Nolan was obliged to suppress his natural impatience and trot quietly down the line to Lieutenant General Sir George de Lacy Evans at the head of the 2nd Division, and then to Lieutenant General Sir George Brown in front of the Light Division. Both Evans and Brown, when passing the order to their own brigadiers, named the far bank of the river as the immediate objective, for neither felt sufficiently informed of the ground and the enemy position to decide what his men should do after they had crossed. The order was specifically not directed to the 1st Division—the second long line—whose ranks remained lying on the ground until the time came to follow in support of the front line— again, in circumstances yet to be decided.

Ten thousand British soldiers rose to their feet and dressed ranks with ceremonial precision. The sergeant majors fussed about as if they were still on the barrack square, calling a file to edge up here or drop back there, while the Russian round shot came bowling up the slope and every few seconds another gap was punched in the splendid, impeccably aligned ranks. Unhappily there was still a flaw in the line, where the 2nd Division's left overlapped the Light Division's right. But apart from that, 10,000 soldiers now stood facing the Russians in a line two miles long and two men deep. There was no attempt to hurry the process of dressing the ranks, for Evans and Brown were both fanatical in their insistence on regimented discipline and none of the officers wanted to risk their displeasure. When at last the process was complete and the divisions were aligned to everybody's satisfaction, a bugle sang out and the British line marched forward in perfect step down the slope toward the river.

At that precise moment, the village of Bourlouik literally went up in flames. The Tatar peasants from the villages and little houses along the riverbank, and the Russian family from the white farmhouse, had fled the day before, when they saw the Russian army taking up its positions on the heights. After they had gone, the Russians made one of their few defensive preparations: they placed quantities of straw in the Bourlouik houses. The skirmishers who were sent forward to fire the village must have waited a long time for the British army finally to make up its mind. But the move forward, when it came, and the firing were almost simultaneous; by the time the brigade on the right of the 2nd Division approached the village, it was burning fiercely. It can be assumed that the Russians set fire to the village to reduce the cover the houses would offer, since they were little more than shacks and would not take much rebuilding. So the burning of Bourlouik hardly indicates a scorched-earth policy, particularly as the nearby bridge over the river was left intact.

The two brigadiers of the 2nd Division were Brigadier General Adams, commanding the right brigade, and Brigadier General Pennefather, commanding the left. The battalions making up Adams' brigade, in the customary listing from right to left, were the Forty-first Regiment (the Welsh Regiment) on the extreme right, the Forty-ninth (the Royal Berkshire Regiment) and the Forty-seventh (the North Lancashire Regi-

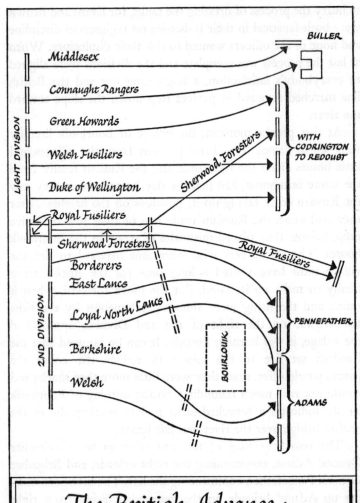

The British Advance:
(2nd and Light Divisions)

ment, or Loyal North Lancs). It was this brigade that was faced with the burning village of Bourlouik, and as it marched forward it was compelled to divide—the Forty-first and Forty-ninth swinging off to the right, led by Adams himself, and the Forty-seventh crowding up against Pennefather's brigade on the left.

An advance in line made shoulder to shoulder, under fire, is difficult enough. When part of the line is deflected by an obstacle, advance becomes even more difficult. Troops moving in relatively loose formations will make their own adjustments to pass around something in their way. But when soldiers are drilled to such a pitch of precision that they must always maintain dressing and spacing, confusion is bound to result from any attempt to compress extra men into a given space. Pennefather's battalions were already marching shoulder to shoulder; the Thirtieth (the East Lancashire Regiment) on the right, the Fifty-fifth (the Border Regiment) in the center, and the Ninety-fifth (the Nottingham and Derby Regiment, known as the Sherwood Foresters) on the left. A brigade front was made up of some 1,200 men and covered almost half a mile. So the Forty-seventh, the Loyal North Lancs ("the Loyals") on the left of Adams' brigade, added another 400 files to Pennefather's already crowded front when they inclined left to avoid Bourlouik—each man, on the word of command, making a forty-five-degree turn so that the line bore leftward, crabwise, but still remained parallel with the front. The result was that the men along the whole length of Pennefather's brigade were pushed towards their left. When a round shot punched a gap in the line, it was almost welcomed, to ease the pressure. When the soldiers were lying down, merely waiting, they had been able to feel distress at what was happening to their more unlucky comrades, but now that they were on the move, each man's thoughts were only of himself and of the immediate demands being made on him. Even nervous thoughts of the enemy ahead were crowded out by the constant problems of dressing and alignment.

It will be remembered that when the 2nd Division extended into line it had to move forward so that its left could overlap the Light Division's right. Consequently the Ninety-fifth, the Sherwood Foresters, on the left of Pennefather's brigade, had become the extreme left of this half of the line, and the officers of that regiment, embarrassed because their men were covering up the Seventh Regiment (the Royal Fusiliers) who were on the right of the Light Division line, were determined to trespass no farther to the left and took more than usual pains to hold their men to an undeviating course. So the Loyals, in avoiding Bourlouik, pressed the East Lancashires away to the left; the East Lancashires pressed the Borderers; the Borderers, in their turn, pressed against the Sherwood Foresters; but the Sherwood Foresters were determined not to be shifted, and soon they and the Borderers were hopelessly entangled.

Although the line of Pennefather's brigade, now lengthened by the Loyals, extended over half a mile, the sector of the front on which it was moving forward, while relatively narrow, was covered by the greatest possible concentration of Russian artillery. This was the only sector on which all the guns could be brought to bear at once—the batteries on Kourganie Hill and those astride the road and on Telegraph Height. Other parts of the front were covered by Russian guns, but only by those guns that actually overlooked the armies. For example, the two battalions that passed to the right of the village—all that was left of Adams' brigade, now that the Loyals had moved over to the left—felt nothing like the impact of artillery that was concentrated on Pennefather's brigade.

Whatever the weight of the fire, both brigades were assailed by a catholic selection of round shot, canister, grapeshot, and musket balls—and still the lines marched on shoulder to shoulder, meticulously preserving the dressing. When they neared the riverbank, the way was barred by walls dividing the gardens, by rows of vines and deep furrows, and by occasional buildings, and the men were forced to break ranks to move forward at all. With mechanical instinct they formed ranks again as soon as they had passed an obstacle, closing up to the first man they could find, picking up dressing, picking up step, although the actual companies and even the battalions were now inevitably becoming mixed. But the British soldier had long been trained to march in line, shoulder to shoulder with the man next to him, and if anything he was discouraged from taking the initiative to move forward individually. He had to form part of a rank, even if it were only a dozen or half a dozen files long; otherwise he was immobilized. And although in the march down to the riverbank the divisional line repeatedly snapped—at some points it broke into fragments—line formation was still maintained in essence, and the soldiers kept advancing shoulder to shoulder.

By now the Russian gunners were not having it all their own way. Evans' batteries had moved forward with his division; they had reduced the range by nearly half a mile and now were drawn up behind Bourlouik, giving the Russians the first taste of British round shot. They were joined by two more batteries of the Royal Horse Artillery, which some enterprising officer sent galloping up from the divisions standing in the rear. Each field gun was drawn by four—sometimes six—horses, with a driver crouched forward on the near-side horse of each pair, belaboring its flanks. The sight of a battery of guns bumping over uneven turf—the horses stretched at full gallop, the limbers thrown up onto one wheel almost to the point of over-balancing, then crashing back again onto the other wheel—was one of the most exhilarating spectacles of nineteenth-century war. Soon there were eighteen guns in battery firing at the Russians, and where but a few minutes before a state of stagnation seemed to have come over the battlefield, now, on the sector between Bourlouik and the bridge, all was movement and gun flashes and sharp cries from men coming into action by the river—although toward the west the French were still waiting in their same positions.

The Light Division on the 2nd Division's left, and just out of alignment with it because of the overlap, moved forward at the same time. The right brigade of the Light Division was under General Codrington—he on the white horse—with the Seventh Regiment (the Royal Fusiliers) on its right. Then came the Thirty-third (the Duke of Wellington's Regiment, from the West Riding of Yorkshire) and the Twenty-third (the Royal Welsh Fusiliers). The left brigade was under General Buller: the Nineteenth (the Yorkshire Regiment, or Green Howards) on its right, next the Eighty-eighth (the Connaught Rangers), and then the Seventy-seventh (the Middlesex Regiment).

The Seventh, the Royal Fusiliers, on the right of the division, was the regiment overlapped by the Ninety-fifth, the Sherwood Foresters. As shown by its numerical annotation, the Seventh was one of the oldest regiments in the British army and had been formed as the City of London Regiment by King James II in 1685. It had been the first regiment to be equipped, at that time, with the "fusil," the flintlock musket, and for that reason King James had honored it with the name, Royal Fusiliers. Since then, of course, the flintlock had been superseded by the percussion cap, but only now were the regiment's muskets being gradually replaced by the new Minié rifle. In the Crimea, it was commanded by Lieutenant Colonel Lacy Yea (he pronounced it Yaw), an officer bursting with energy and drive, who believed his regiment and the men in it to be far superior to any other unit of the British army. It is not unusual for a commanding officer to hold that belief, but to Yea it was more than conventional pride, it was a rabid conviction that led him to behave with an impressive individuality. He had not taken with very good grace the masking of his regiment by the Sherwood Foresters, but he was a good enough soldier to keep his men in their proper position in the divisional line and to bide his time until the opportunity should come to lead them to the front of the battle.

The opportunity came soon enough. The lines reached the gardens and were soon broken up when the men had to climb walls or take temporary cover in furrows and behind buildings. Repeatedly, little groups of soldiers formed improvised ranks, making short dashes forward from one piece of cover to another, and in the consequent disorder the Borderers and the Sherwood Foresters became hopelessly mixed. Yea, following behind the Sherwood Foresters with his Fusiliers, could see the chaos ahead and, stepping out directly toward it, he ordered his regiment to follow him straight through the disordered ranks on the left of Pennefather's brigade.

He might have added to the confusion and become enmeshed in it himself had his Fusiliers not been such a highly disciplined and homogeneous unit. Moreover, he had found a legitimate soldier's excuse for breaking away from the rigid line of the Light Division, and thereafter he led his Royal Fusiliers on their own direct course down to the river. One of his men, Timothy Gowing, was later to write, "To describe my feelings in going into action I could not. As soon as the enemy's round shot came hopping along we simply did the polite—opened up and allowed them to pass on; there is nothing lost by politeness, even on a battlefield. As we kept advancing, we had to move our pins to get out of the way. . . . Up to the river we rushed and got ready for a swim, pulling off knapsacks and camp kettles. A number of our poor fellows were drowned, or shot down with grape and canister—which came amongst us like hail—while attempting to cross. Into the river we dashed, nearly up to our armpits, with our ammunition and rifles at the top of our heads to keep them dry, scrambled out the best way we could—the banks were very steep and slippery—and commenced to ascend the hill."

The Fusiliers were not actually the first British troops over the river that afternoon—that honor went to Colonel Stacey and a few men of the Loyals—but they were the first full battalion to cross as one unit. Inevitably they were considerably disorganized; their companies were mixed; but they were still together, as one unit, following their colonel. Whether by artifice or by accident, Yea had succeeded in detaching his Fusiliers from Codrington's brigade, and he was now left to act independently in assaulting the Russian positions.

On the other hand, the Sherwood Foresters—when they had disentangled themselves from the Borderers and were no longer concerned that they were masking the Fusiliers, who had passed right through—began to veer over to the left to avoid further entanglements. Thus they lost touch with their own brigade entirely and fought the rest of the battle as part of Codrington's brigade, in fact as part of the Light Division, to which they did not belong.

So the Light Division on the left, almost immediately after it started moving forward, lost the Seventh, the Royal Fusiliers, and gained the Ninety-fifth, the Sherwood Foresters. The Sherwood Foresters, free at last of their entanglements and seeking a gap in the line into which they could insert themselves, passed right behind the other two battalions in Codrington's brigade and worked themselves into position on the left of the Twenty-third, the Royal Welsh Fusiliers. The three battalions now making up Codrington's brigade were the Thirty-third, the Duke of Wellington's; the Twenty-third, the Royal Welsh Fusiliers; and the Ninety-fifth, the Sherwood Foresters. On their left, Buller's brigade still consisted of the Nineteenth, the Green Howards; the Eighty-eighth, the Connaught Rangers; and the Seventy-seventh, the Middlesex Regiment.

All the battalions that now made up the Light Division line marched down toward the river behind Sir George Brown, who could see such a short way ahead that he had no idea of what he would do when he reached it. The division formed the extreme left of the allied line. The attention of the Russian batteries was drawn mainly to the 2nd Division as it approached the river in the central sector half a mile above and below the bridge, so the Light Division was not so harassed by artillery fire. Nevertheless, as the two slender ranks came down into the vineyards, they were assailed by a hail of musket fire from sharpshooters lying out in front of the Russian columns on the opposite bank. But musket fire—and even rifle fire at that stage of its development—was remarkably inaccurate. The likelihood of being hit depended more on chance than marksmanship even though the long ranks presented such a wide target, if only because the powder charges varied so much in strength that no two shots followed the same trajectory. All the same, some of the fire found its victims.

The soldiers of the Light Division were faced with the same hazards and obstacles in going through the vineyards as those that were troubling their comrades in the 2nd—walls to be climbed, ditches to be jumped, vines to be avoided—but Sir George Brown's men suffered many fewer casualties than did Pennefather's brigade. The battalions and the companies had to break their line to pass the obstacles, and then regroup, but when they actually reached the river they were generally in their correct formation.

When he came to the river, Sir George Brown found a reasonably shallow crossing. The conditions for the rest of the division varied along its line. Some of the men had to wade only up to their ankles; a few found themselves waist-deep, even breast-high, in the water, holding their muskets and ammunition above their heads and feeling forward gingerly for each step lest the river bottom plunge even deeper. A few were caught off guard and fell into deep holes, borne down by the weight of their equipment. They struggled wildly—floundering, clawing their neighbors, some actually drowning. Others were shot down; some wounded men drowned in shallow water. A few found cover behind the bank of a vineyard or the wall of a house and never came down to the river at all, unable to summon the will to face a second time the frightening new experience of openly inviting death.

Except at one place where the stream writhes through an S-bend, the reach of river along which the Light Division was extended is comparatively straight, and on the far side runs a narrow ledge—not more than a few yards wide—from which a sheer bank rises some ten to fifteen feet, along nearly the whole length of the division's front. The ground above the bank slopes up quite gently towards the Great Redoubt—no more than 400 yards away. The Russian guns in the Redoubt commanded the whole slope, and as soon as any troops climbed to the top of the bank they would find themselves in direct line of an almost point-blank cannon fire.

But so long as the troops remained huddled along the ledge below the bank they were almost entirely screened from enemy fire; nearly 5,000 men crowded into this narrow shelter. Some of the more adventurous Russian sharpshooters crept forward to the lip of the bank to take snap shots into the mass of British infantry below. The casualties they inflicted were painful enough but not large-scale, because the Russians could only show their heads momentarily over the edge of the bank, while they took their aim, and then had to dart back quickly out of sight.

The bank starts to drop away in front of the place where General Buller's brigade—the left-hand brigade of the division—was located, until it vanishes altogether in front of the position taken by the Seventy-seventh, the Middlesex Regiment, on the absolute left of the allied armies. The troops faced a rising stretch of open ground that runs up towards the eastern slopes of Kourganie Hill. There was nothing between the Seventy-seventh and any enemy that might bear down upon the flank, and Buller swung the battalion around to face the left, ordering the men to lie down on the ground and wait. He formed the next battalion, the Connaught Rangers, into a hollow square, its front facing up the hillside. The bank rises in front of the spot on which his most rightward battalion, the Green Howards, stood, and they consequently found themselves in the same situation as the battalions of Codrington's brigade. Actually, they joined that brigade when it climbed the bank to go forward. But General Buller himself, feeling the weight of responsibility devolving on the troops guarding the left of the allied line, remained with the other two battalions.

9

INTO THE REDOUBT

THE COMMISSIONED and noncommissioned officers of Codrington's brigade fussed up and down the lines, trying to find some resemblance to the ordered units to which they were accustomed. But the ledge was narrow, and to make conditions more difficult it was littered with boulders and branches of trees that had been left by the river when it came down in flood. Inevitably there had been some misplacement of units during the passage of the vineyards and the river crossing. The lack of order and alignment, the impossibility of dressing and covering off the ranks properly, annoyed Sir George Brown almost beyond endurance. Worse still, there was hardly any room for him and his staff, determined to achieve order, to move their horses between the sinuous lines of soldiers and the vertical bank. Sir George fussed about until he found a place where the bank had been broken away slightly, so that he was able to put his horse to it and scramble up to the top. It was an act of sheer exasperation. For all his short-sightedness Sir George must have known what he was risking, but it was not necessarily as heroic a gesture as it appeared.

It was more than forty years since Sir George had been in

action. In the meantime his military activities had been confined to drilling and disciplining his troops, activities which he no longer looked on as a means to military efficiency that might some day be valuable in battle, but as an end in themselves. For him, drill and discipline were the ultimate objects of soldiering; fighting was merely incidental.

Sir George was still determined to get his division decently aligned, and as he sat on his charger on top of the bank, the plumes of his cocked hat waving as much from his own agitation as from the breeze, he shouted order after order, although nobody could really hear. For some reason the Russians seemed not to be firing at him—he was a target that could hardly be missed—but the terrifying sight of the infuriated figure on the charger had sent the sharpshooters back to their columns.

Two Russian columns stood flanking the Great Redoubt at an angle, one on each side, like two barriers placed to force approaching traffic to converge toward one point. It was not the practice of Russian infantry when drawn up in column to open fire until they were engaged directly with the enemy, and when the sharpshooters withdrew no fire came from the columns flanking the Redoubt. The big guns were still directing their fire towards Pennefather's brigade and the sector down-river where the 2nd Division was making its crossing. So far there had been no indication to the Russians, except for the surprising figure of Sir George Brown, that the British troops who had made their way over the river were ready to climb the bank and start the final assault, so the gunners had not yet lowered their sights to open their point-blank fire on attackers coming up the slope in front of them.

General Codrington crossed the river lower down than did Sir George Brown and reached the south bank between the Duke of Wellington's Regiment and the Royal Welsh Fusiliers

—the two battalions which now seemed to mark the extreme right of the Light Division. Colonel Yea and his Royal Fusiliers, after passing through the Sherwood Foresters, had moved quite a distance to the right, so they could no longer be regarded as under Codrington's control—although in reality they were still under his command. Here, at the end of the Light Division line, the river makes a couple of violent twists; not only would it have been a forlorn hope to attempt to straighten out the line but at the same time it was impossible to see what was happening more than a short way either up or down the river. Indeed, Codrington had not seen Sir George Brown mount the bank.

The orders given to all the brigadiers when the advance began had been merely to take their battalions across the river. The four brigades making up the two divisions were still part of the same line, so the brigadiers could reasonably expect that new orders, to co-ordinate the next moves of their brigades, would be forthcoming when they reached the other bank. But the two battalions on the right of Codrington's brigade were dangerously crowded; it was imperative to make some move quickly. The only move that could be made was forward, up the bank. As if to impress on the British the need to get away quickly from the narrow river ledge, a group of Russian skirmishers lurking on the empty stretch between Codrington's right and Yea's Fusiliers opened an enfilading fire into the crowded ranks of the Royal Welsh Fusiliers.

Codrington had never been in action before, nor had he come out to the East as part of the Light Division. He was a Guardsman of the Coldstream and a man of considerable means, like most officers of the British army. Impatient that he had not been drafted with the Guards' battalions that had been sent to Turkey, he had traveled out at his own expense and presented himself to Lord Raglan at Varna, asking to be employed in the war. When Raglan gave him a brigade he became something of a rarity—a Guards officer commanding a brigade of the Line. In the British army, the Guards and the Line existed in separate worlds: the Guards believed themselves to dwell on a far higher plane and occasionally even refused to fight along-side the Line.

Codrington, for all his lack of battle experience, saw im-mediately that his brigade could not stay down on the ledge. Like Sir George Brown, he found a place where he could scramble up the bank on his white Arab pony. He shouted, in competition with the gunfire, "Fix bayonets! Get up the bank and advance!" But he was wearing an ordinary forage cap rather than the usual brigadier's cocked hat with flowing plumes, because he had not come out to the East equipped as a general officer. Consequently the soldiers massed down below did not easily recognize him as their brigadier; the men were never ready to be deflected by orders given by anyone except their own company commanders, unless they were overawed by the trappings of high authority. A general in a cocked hat demanded spontaneous obedience; an ordinary-looking officer who was not of their own regiment could be regarded with a certain amount of suspicion.

However, Codrington managed to gather some followers, and a few men started to scramble up the bank. He rode his horse forward a few yards and they followed him; then he stopped to look back, waving and telling them to call some more. In a series of short forward rushes, each time with a few more adherents, he started to draw the men of his brigade for-ward, and soon they were all scrambling up the bank—the Duke of Wellington's, the Royal Welsh Fusiliers, and the Green Howards from Buller's brigade.

Almost at the same time, but quite separately and spontaneously—because he had detached himself from Codrington's brigade—Colonel Yea gave a similar lead to his Fusiliers. The companies and platoons in his battalion had been badly mixed up during their encounter with the Sherwood Foresters, and he was finding it fruitless to try and sort out the confusion on the narrow ledge below the bank. He too was soon on top of the bank, shouting, "Never mind forming! Come along anyhow!"—an almost unprecedented order. But because they knew him well, his men obeyed without hesitation, and the Royal Fusiliers were among the first of the British soldiers up the bank.

So the whole Light Division that had survived the march down to the river and the crossing, except Buller's two battalions watching the left of the army, was soon upon the long slope leading straight to the Great Redoubt, where the gunners were lowering their sights and bringing down the muzzles of their cannon to point at this incredible target—not 400 yards away and reducing the range every minute.

By the time some 4,000 men clawed their way up the bank, kicking away the edges in their scramble, calling to their comrades who had already reached the top for a hand up, there was little or no regimental order left. Sir George Brown was almost apoplectic. The officers and the sergeants, driven by their instinct and training as much as by their sense of Sir George's displeasure, blandly ignored the imminence of the enemy and hustled about trying to get the men to make up some sort of line formation, even though it was impossible in the circumstances to sort out the companies. But Codrington was still riding forward, drawing more and more men after him, and it began to dawn on all ranks that the need for alignment was being disregarded even by authority; now that the division had actually gained the slope there was only one purpose—to reach the Great Redoubt. Perhaps order would be restored when they got there, but meanwhile even colonels and brigadiers were urging them on in a most irregular manner.

On both sides of what had now become a shapeless mass of soldiery stood the Russian columns that were disposed at an angle to the Great Redoubt—each column with 1,500 men drawn up in eight ranks. Some of the Russian soldiers in the front ranks raised their muskets and fired at random into the groups of British soldiers, but the firing was uncontrolled and virtually unaimed. It was the Russian practice to put the men with longer service in the outside ranks and to pack the body of the column with newer recruits. The recruits were even less controlled, and they fired their muskets into the air (they could hardly fire into the backs of the rank in front); altogether the firing made a lot of noise, but it had little effect. The Green Howards, who found themselves nearest to the Russian column on the left, started firing into this mass of gray-coated figures. Soon the Green Howards were shooting with keen deliberation, almost as if it were a sport, and men from other battalions came over to the left to join in. Before long, as the Russians in the outside ranks started to fall, the column began to move ponderously away toward the eastern slopes of Kourganie Hill, leaving behind a score of inert figures sprawled on the ground.

On the other flank, the Royal Fusiliers were facing the corresponding Russian column, but here there was no random shooting. As soon as Yea brought his men up onto the slope, he determined to get them into companies and into line. Above all the din that was going on, he shouted orders and imprecations, he pushed men here and cursed them there, until he had some semblance of a battalion drawn up in two ranks. He wheeled the ranks to face directly at the Russian column, not

[117]

a hundred yards away, and as soon as they were thus drawn up a fight started that was to last for half an hour and be an epic on its own. (We shall come back to Yea and the Royal Fusiliers, and their fight with the Kazan Regiment.)

Now that the men of the Light Division were on the slope in their hundreds, the guns in the Great Redoubt opened a devastatingly direct fire. For the next ten minutes, as what looked like a riotous mob surged forward toward the Redoubt, the guns fired salvo after salvo of canister and round shot, each salvo driving a swath of destruction through the oncoming soldiers, who were crowding closer together every minute. A round shot could mow down and kill half a dozen men if they were standing bunched in its path, particularly at that short range, and the guns created havoc wherever they found a target. But even so, many pressed on up the slope quite un-scathed, mainly because the Russian column on the left had been driven away and Yea's battalion was drawing all the fire from the column on the right. So, at any rate at first, there was relatively litle musket fire directed against the main mass, and the damage caused by each shot from one of the big guns was always localized.

As the foremost attackers approached the Redoubt, now almost entirely obscured by thick smoke from the guns, a company of Russian infantrymen climbed the mound of earth that had been piled up in rear of the emplacement and started pouring a heavy musket fire over the heads of the gunners, to add to the fire already assailing the Light Division. But the division still came on, at the heels of Codrington's white pony, more like a force of buccaneers than a disciplined military formation.

The whole intention of placing the Russian columns at an angle, flanking each side of the Redoubt, had been that they should act as a funnel, sucking the attackers in toward the center, toward the guns; and that was the effect. Although the four battalions of the Light Division made no pretense of alignment when they climbed up from the river, they had covered a front of nearly three quarters of a mile. As they pressed forward up the slope, their front contracted; now, close to the Redoubt, it was compressed to less than 400 yards, hardly longer than the length of the Redoubt itself. Not any more was it even the pretense of a military line; it was a seething mass of attacking soldiers, and although it was still raked by musket fire and round shot, nothing could stop it from reaching its objective.

All at once, the guns stopped firing. For a few minutes a curtain of thick smoke hung over the forward edge of the Redoubt, until a slight breeze slowly rolled it away. As the smoke dispersed, the Russians were seen to be limbering up their guns, hitching each to a team of twelve horses and hurrying them away to the rear. The attackers still had the last hundred yards to cover, and many of the British soldiers were feeling the effects of the tremendous exertions they had made during the last half hour. But General Codrington, miraculously unscathed, put his pony hard at the earth mound banked up in front of the Redoubt and pulled up short on top of the parapet. Snatching off his forage cap and waving it high in the air, in the best manner of the classic military leader, he called on his men to make the last effort to gain the Great Redoubt, even though the Russian infantrymen on the reverse parapet were still keeping up a steady musket fire. A young ensign of the Royal Welsh Regiment sprinted forward with his regiment's Queen's color and thrust the staff into the ground at the top of the mound. Immediately he was shot dead. As he fell the color fell with him, but it was quickly retrieved and hoisted again

by a private of the regiment, and then—because privates were
not normally trusted with colors—was taken over by a corporal
and then a sergeant, and finally, more fittingly, by an officer.

In a few minutes, nearly 2,000 British soldiers were milling
about in the Redoubt and on the ground close below, and the
company of Russian infantrymen had departed from the
reverse parapet. But the price had been high. More than 300
dead and wounded lay on the slope. The wounded lay untended, and the battle was to pass over them twice again,
fiercely fought, before anybody was to come to their succor.

10

OUT FROM THE REDOUBT

MEANWHILE, General Prince Napoleon was acquiring, through his inactivity, the military reputation that was to dog him for the rest of his life. Perhaps it is a little unfair that he suffered from the events of the day more than the other French generals; although Bosquet and Canrobert did take their divisions to the enemy side of the river, neither led his troops into active combat with the Russians.

Subsequent accounts of the battle published in France certainly suggested that Bosquet's and Canrobert's divisions were involved in some epic engagements. These accounts were highly imaginative—even in some respects entirely imaginary. They gave the other two generals credit for having engaged the enemy but at the same time pointed out that Prince Napoleon had kept his division safely out of contact with the Russians—which is, of course, the inescapable truth. But by three o'clock in the afternoon, at the various points where St. Arnaud had intended his divisions to make their crossings, the whole French army was in a state of utter stagnation.

At the river mouth, the brigade under General Bouat that

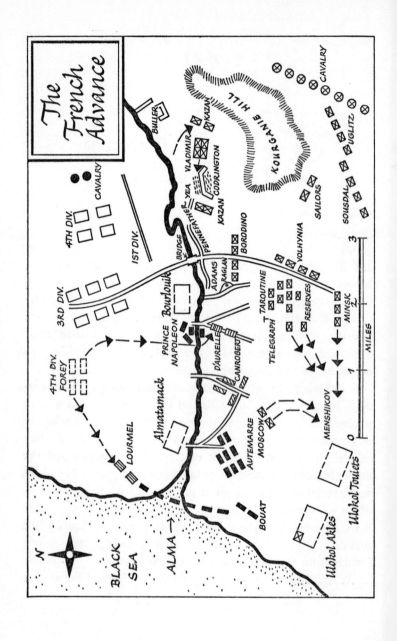

The French Advance

had been sent to climb the path up the cliffs was still involved in its laborious exercise. The first companies had reached the top of the cliff and were being drawn up on the plateau in their columns, but because Bouat had not been able to bring his guns over the sand bar and had sent them round to Bosquet, he was now in that irresolute state of a French infantry commander who believes himself powerless to act without artillery. In any case, since Menshikov had withdrawn from Ulukol Touiets—and had incidentally taken away with him the Minsk Battalion that had originally been posted at Ulukol Akles—Bouat was still two and a half miles from the nearest Russian formation. By now the directing of 12,000 soldiers to this part of the field seemed utterly fruitless. To add to the futility, St. Arnaud had moved to Bouat's support a complete brigade from General Forey's 4th Division—the only unit of the French army left in reserve. The brigade was commanded by General Lourmel, and Forey rode with him almost as a supernumerary. They marched down to the mouth of the river, waited there in the queue to cross the sand bar—and were still waiting when the Battle of the Alma was over.

A mile upriver, overlooking Almatamack, Bosquet, with Autemarre's brigade, was still immobile. Having gained the plateau, he had been waiting at the top of the road for almost an hour. Bosquet had four batteries of guns with him. But he, too, was a mile and a half from the nearest Russian formation. Earlier in the afternoon, when Bosquet first appeared on the plateau, Kiriakov had moved two battalions of the Moscow Regiment toward him, but these were taken away by Menshikov on his impetuous dash to the west. It is easy to conclude that Bosquet showed a lamentable lack of initiative by failing to order Autemarre's brigade to advance across the plateau towards the Russians, even though they were such a

[123]

long way away. After all, the whole purpose for which St.
Arnaud had sent Bosquet's division to cross the lower reach of
the river was to attack the left of the Russian position. If
Bosquet felt that Autemarre's brigade was too weak, even
though it was supported by guns, he could well have called
some of Bouat's men across to strengthen it—there was less
than a mile of open plateau between them. Perhaps Bosquet
believed that he must leave Bouat and all his men on the cliff
in case the Russians from Ulukol Akles tried to work round the
flank. But a force of 12,000 men, now being reinforced by
Lourmel's brigade, seems excessive to guard a flank threatened
by only one battalion.

When Bosquet faced the river crossing and ascended the
ravine, where he might well have been ambushed, he showed
his acknowledged gift of enterprising generalship. It would
have been wholly in character if this veteran of so many
Algerian campaigns had then set off boldly across the plateau to
search out the enemy. So it can only be inferred that when St.
Arnaud ordered him to use his division to turn the enemy left,
Bosquet fully expected to find himself faced by the Russians
as soon as he reached the top of the cliff and never contemplated
a long march on the enemy's side of the river before coming
into action. He knew that Canrobert's division was crossing the
river only a mile higher up; perhaps when he saw the actual
situation on the plateau he decided that the enemy positions
were so far away that, if anybody was to attack them, it
should be Canrobert, who was much nearer. He was unaware
that Canrobert had immobilized himself while waiting for his
guns to go round by Almatamack.

By three o'clock, only four battalions of Prince Napoleon's
division had crossed the river—the Nineteenth Chasseurs, a
battalion of the Marine Corps, and two battalions of the Second

Zouave Regiment. It soon became clear to the Zouave officers that their divisional commander had little enthusiasm for seeking out the enemy, so, without hesitation, as soon as they were across the river, they marched their two battalions—2,000 men —away to the right, along the river ledge, until they came to the ravine up which Canrobert's division was waiting. There they climbed the ravine and placed themselves alongside the First Zouaves on Canrobert's left. By their own decision, without reference to higher authority, the Second Zouaves thus left the 3rd Division and joined the 1st.

This reduced Prince Napoleon's division to 5,000 men, broken up into their individual battalions of which, apart from the Zouaves, only two had actually crossed the river. These battalions were both waiting on the river ledge, huddled up under the shelter of the hills rising in front of them. Even had they felt impelled to advance up the road that climbed the hills from the point where they had forded the river, they could not have moved forward because this road was hopelessly blocked.

St. Arnaud could see that Prince Napoleon's 3rd Division halted when it came down to the river; to his untrained mind the only remedy that suggested itself was to throw in more men. He had divided Forey's division—sending one brigade, under General Lourmel, down to the river mouth as we have seen—so he ordered the other brigade, under General d'Aurelle, to join Prince Napoleon. This senseless order would add 3,500 infantrymen to the congestion already caused by six battalions trying to cross the river under fire at one narrow ford, in the same apparently purposeless manner in which the other brigade of Forey's division was increasing the confusion at the sand bar.

Thus was St. Arnaud to dissipate his entire tactical reserve.

[1 2 5]

His whole army was now committed to cross the river at one or another of the four points; if the forces at one of these points were to fall into difficulties and need assistance, there was not a company left to be sent to their help. Methods of communication between units of an army in those days were so ineffectual that it would have been almost impossible for St. Arnaud to draw off an individual battalion, or even a brigade, once he had committed it to movement as part of a division. In any case St. Arnaud, surrounded by the battalions of Prince Napoleon's division milling around in their search for cover from enemy artillery fire, was quite cut off from contact with his divisional generals and had no idea of the course of the battle as a whole.

But d'Aurelle's brigade did not join the queue of Prince Napoleon's battalions waiting to cross the river. D'Aurelle had his own interpretation of the order given to him to support the 3rd Division. When he saw how most of the battalions of that division were concentrated in amorphous groups, still in the vineyards on the north side of the river, he decided to bypass them. He marched his own men to the river a short way downstream and, by chance, found a point where the river was easily forded: his whole brigade crossed without difficulty and with little interference from enemy fire. Then he swung to the left, back along the river ledge, until he came to the road up which Prince Napoleon's men were supposed to be advancing, but from which they were still hanging back. He marched his brigade, a column half a mile long, into the roadway, and when they were all on the road he halted to await further orders. Of course no orders came, because neither Prince Napoleon nor even St. Arnaud had any idea that the brigade was there. But the Chasseurs and the Marine Corps, the only battalions of the 3rd Division other than the Zouaves that were over the river, found the road blocked by d'Aurelle's brigade.

They seemed quite content to use this as a justification for remaining stationary.

The battle was thus the reverse of St. Arnaud's plan: the units from the right did not attack progressively and draw off the Russians, so that the British army on the left could make the final assault; rather, the British made the opening attack on the left while the French units on the right held back.

At the time Lord Raglan gave the order to advance, he and his staff had been at the extreme right of the British line where, to move clear of the British 2nd Division, they had ridden into the space between the British and French armies. It had been the intention that the armies should be in touch with each other to form a continuous front, but the vicissitudes of the march had not allowed things to work out that way, and the space between them had alternately widened and closed. Now there was almost a quarter of a mile between the right of Evans' division and the left of Prince Napoleon's. It was only because Adams' brigade had to incline right to avoid Bourlouik that this gap had been narrowed at all; it was never entirely closed. The weakest part of the whole front therefore was the absolute center, a weakness that could have been disastrous had it been exploited by the Russians.

Raglan instinctively moved forward with his army, but unlike St. Arnaud he stayed apart from any of his divisions. He had moved in the spheres of high command for so long that he automatically kept himself aloof and would never have allowed himself to be engulfed by his subordinates. But that does not mean he was content to hold himself back from places where the men under his command were in action. When the British troops moved forward, he rode down toward the river with them, parallel to the end of the advancing line but

[127]

borne away to the right by the two battalions of Adams'
brigade that had to swing to the right to avoid Bourlouik. Here,
the enemy's artillery fire was relatively light. Most of the fire
was being concentrated on Pennefather's brigade on the left
of the 2nd Division, around and just above the bridge.

When Raglan's little party reached the river, they soon
found an easy crossing, about half a mile down from the bridge.
The stream was flowing strongly, but some rocks wedged on
the river bottom had formed a little dam which held back a
considerable pool. Although the horse of one staff officer
stumbled dangerously, Raglan's brown bay easily picked his
way over; and Raglan was the first of the party to reach the
opposite bank—probably only a very few minutes after the first
of the infantry higher upstream. Downstream below the dam,
within a few yards, French skirmishers on the left of Prince
Napoleon's division were exchanging fire with Russian sharpshooters who had been placed in some thick foliage at the
bottom of the hill falling from Telegraph Height. The group
of horsemen offered an easy target to the Russian sharpshooters, and two of Raglan's staff were hit, although neither
was killed. The Frenchmen showed some natural surprise at a
posse of staff officers with cocked hats riding forward, apparently in actual advance of their own front line. They could
only infer that the British army had already crossed the river
higher upstream; word to that effect was soon passed down and
did in fact reach St. Arnaud.

Raglan, on reaching the other side, rode off impulsively toward the right, but one of his staff shouted, "This seems a
better way, my lord!" In actual fact the officer had no better
knowledge of the ground than Raglan, and it was quite fortui-
tous that he led the way up a path that bore off toward the
left and took the staff to a heaven-sent point of vantage. They

climbed steeply, although the horses took it in easy stride, and almost immediately emerged onto the crest of the western side of the wide ravine up the middle of which ran the Sebastopol road. The path, in effect, led to the heart of the Russian positions. Not many minutes before, one of the Taroutine battalions had rested beside it before withdrawing farther up Telegraph Height.

When the riders had traveled up the path for nearly half a mile, they came to a ledge that protruded from the side of the hill overlooking the ravine. It was a wide, almost semicircular knoll, rather like a pulpit, standing out obtrusively from the hill behind it. Raglan recognized it at once as an ideal position from which to view at least the British sector of the battlefield. On this knoll, as he sat his horse, he faced due east and could see before him the whole line of river above the bridge where the British were about to cross. Before him too, straight ahead, were the Great Redoubt and the Russian positions on the slopes of Kourganie Hill. And almost directly below him, not a quarter of a mile away, were some of the Russian battalions and batteries astride the road. Ahead, his view was unrestricted, but the rising ground to the right swung forward to obscure his view of the road to the south; to the left, he could see nothing of the river below the bridge; nor, of course, could he see anything toward the west, because the slopes of Telegraph Height rose directly behind him.

Believers in the modern principle of making commanding generals as inconspicuous as possible will be horrified at the idea of the whole staff taking up prominent positions, virtually in the heart of the enemy line, and advertising those positions with a bevy of cocked hats and plumes. But Raglan was determined to profit from his lucky discovery of this ideal vantage point.

"Our presence here will have the best effect," he said—

implying that he wanted the enemy to see him and his staff and thereby get the impression that all the ground to the west, which was hidden as much from the Russians on the Kourganie slopes as it was from Raglan himself, was in allied hands—"Now! If we had a couple of guns up here!"

An artillery officer hurried away, down the hill, back across the river, to General Adams. Adams detached two guns; the teams were sent cantering down to the ford that Raglan had found, and without any interference from the enemy they too appeared on the knoll to establish an artillery emplacement right in the heart of the enemy position. They reached the knoll just as Codrington's brigade was forging its way up the slope toward the Great Redoubt, and there is no doubt that the two guns under the direct orders of the commander in chief were able—thanks, in this instance, to their elevated position—to cause considerable damage to the battery in the Redoubt and have a marked influence on the Russians' decision to remove their guns altogether.

Just at the moment when Codrington was making his final assault, a French aide-de-camp came hurrying up the path to find Raglan, proving that the British staff's movement had been quickly reported to the French commander in chief. The French officer approaching Raglan on foot—it may be that his horse had been shot from under him as he crossed the river—was bareheaded, disheveled, and panting. He blurted out, "My lord, my lord! We have before us eight battalions!"

He gave no further explanation of what he meant: who it was that was faced by eight battalions, or why it should be so critical for any force to have eight battalions in front of it.

Raglan might well have pointed out that the British were facing at least sixteen. However, he said to the Frenchman, "I could spare you a battalion." Apparently the man was satisfied, because he hurried away. Raglan did not follow up his offer. Nor can he really be blamed, because he had not been told where or by whom the relief was wanted.

The eight battalions that were disturbing the French command were the force which Menshikov had marched across to Ulukol Touiets and then sent marching all the way back again. They consisted of three battalions of the Minsk Regiment, drawn from the main reserve on the road, and four battalions of the Moscow Regiment that had been taken from their positions on the top of Telegraph Height. To these Menshikov had added the detached battalion of the Minsk Regiment which had originally been posted at Ulukol Akles. Assembling the eight battalions in one mass, in two parallel columns of four battalions each, he had marched them about the plateau in this solid group like a ship tacking, first in one direction and then another. After finally ordering them back from Ulukol Touiets, he rode ahead and waited for them at the top of Telegraph Height. While he was waiting he learned that two French columns, in addition to Bosquet's, were crossing the river—one at the white farmhouse and another at a ford half a mile farther up. With the same impulsive haste that had carried him across the plateau when Bosquet's emergence had been reported, he decided to take this double column—about 6,500 men—on a similar expedition to confront the two French divisions that were intruding on the south bank of the river.

But just before the column arrived back from the west, news was brought to Menshikov that the British army had launched its attack. Mercurial as ever, he sent for Kiriakov and handed the eight battalions over to him.

Kiriakov's horse had been shot from under him, and he came on foot. But he took the eight battalions as Menshikov

[1 3 1]

ordered and moved them back across the plateau on a wide arc that started by bearing away from the river and then swung down toward it. He made no contact with Prince Napoleon's division or d'Aurelle's brigade; he never even knew that they were down by the river at the foot of the hills along the crest of which he was marching. Following the arc all the while, he struck the line of river quite by chance at the top of the ravine in which Canrobert's division was waiting.

Kiriakov halted his column on the plateau at the head of the ravine. Hesitating to probe the ravine and perhaps enter a trap, he stood waiting for Canrobert to make the first move. But Canrobert was not ready to fight: he had infantry but still no artillery. Faced with a formidable array of eight battalions, he withdrew the whole of his division, including Prince Napoleon's Zouaves, down onto the river ledge before a shot was fired.

It was Canrobert's situation of which the aide-de-camp had come rushing to inform Lord Raglan. But Raglan was already aware that the French part of the battle had come to nothing, and he was now solely concerned to see his own lines assault the enemy on Kourganie Hill.

The capture of the Great Redoubt by Codrington's brigade may have been spectacular enough, but it was an empty victory for the British—even worse, it placed in a shockingly vulnerable position the disordered crowd of 2,000 soldiers who were milling about.

Colonel Yea and his Fusiliers were still engaged with the two Kazan battalions on the right of the Redoubt; the Fusiliers were holding off these battalions successfully and preventing their swinging around behind the British troops who had crowded forward without any supports in their rear. On the other flank, on the British left, the two Russian battalions had been driven off, mainly by the Green Howards and the Royal Welsh Fusiliers, soon after the first troops had climbed the bank and the assault up the slope had begun. But it was absurd to expect that the enemy had been driven away from that flank altogether, particularly as it was open country and the massed Russian cavalry was waiting very close at hand. Unlike the right flank, where the Fusiliers had virtually set up a protective line, the left was now quite unguarded. General Buller was, indeed, down at the river with two of his battalions, watching the flank, but he could have done little to hold off a Russian attack on Codrington's men 400 yards up the slope.

There was no order of any sort in the Redoubt. The force that stormed the hill, apart from the Royal Fusiliers, was made up of two battalions of Codrington's brigade—the Duke of Wellington's Regiment and the Royal Welsh Fusiliers—and on their left the Sherwood Foresters, who had broken away from Pennefather's brigade and had moved across the rear of these two other battalions. On the left of the Sherwood Foresters were the Green Howards, the one battalion from Buller's brigade on the extreme left of the Light Division that had not remained down by the river bank.

So it was these four battalions—the Duke of Wellington's, the Royal Welsh, the Sherwood Foresters, and the Green Howards—that converged on the narrow front of the Great Redoubt and in so converging and pressing forward became completely mixed up.

After they had climbed the riverbank, the soldiers hesitated, at first, to go forward except in their proper platoons and companies, and keeping their proper alignment. The officers, lacking orders to the contrary, encouraged their hesitation. But Codrington called them on without regard for who they were or to what regiment they belonged, and it soon became evident throughout the ranks that they were expected blindly to rush the Great Redoubt without first regrouping. It was the antithesis of everything the soldiers had been taught, although it has to be remembered that they had hardly been trained for actual fighting. But now that they were facing a murderous enemy fire that plowed great furrows through their ranks, the order to which they had been so strictly confined on the parade ground certainly seemed out of place; there appeared to be nothing wrong in charging blindly ahead, especially since they were being exhorted to do so by their leaders.

Although it was a disordered crowd that swarmed around the Great Redoubt, it was not disorderly. Regiments and companies were inextricably mixed up, but every man behaved with the discipline that was by now second nature. Nevertheless those junior officers who again started trying to collect their own men soon gave it up as hopeless.

The Redoubt was shallow, a hollow in the ground 300 yards long and 10 yards wide, with the earth that had been dug from it piled as a parapet along the front and back. Some of the men who crowded inside lay against the rear parapet and engaged the enemy wherever they could see them. Others stood about, or sat down, or even lay exhausted from the ordeal of charging up the slope carrying full equipment under fire. Soon there were more casualties, because the Russians placed the guns they had removed from the Redoubt in a new position, not a quarter of a mile away, and started firing into the crowd with devastating effect. Men began to climb out over the front parapet, and General Codrington could be seen driving them back, lest they start a widespread movement that would develop into a retreat.

There were 2,000 British soldiers in this isolated pocket at the foot of Kourganie Hill, a quarter of a mile from the river.

Round this disorganized force were some 14,000 Russian infantrymen, disposed at various points in well-ordered columns. But Codrington was sure that the British 1st Division, forming the next line, would soon be coming up the slope in support. He was determined to keep his men inside the Redoubt until their position was consolidated, if only because he realized that they were far safer there than if they were to fall back even for a short distance on the ground sloping down to the river, where the Russians would be able to direct a heavy fire on them from the batteries on both flanks. But there was no sign of any support. The Russians were unlikely to leave the crowd in the Redoubt unmolested for long. Soon indeed there appeared, round a spur of Kourganie Hill, a formidable column made up of four battalions of the Vladimir Regiment, 3,000 strong in all.

After the battle, both General Gorchakov and General Kvetzenski claimed to have led this column in person, although neither would agree that the other had taken any part. Menshikov had gone off without informing his subordinate generals, so Kvetzenski, who commanded the eastern sector, had no reason to guess that Gorchakov was exercising his authority as second-in-command. But Gorchakov had seen that the British 2nd Division, whose attack was directed in the central sector of the front astride the road—Gorchakov's own sector—had not advanced beyond the riverbank, whereas the Light Division on the British left had made its assault on the Great Redoubt. Looking for Menshikov and hearing that he had ridden off to the west, Gorchakov went over to Kvetzenski's sector; but instead of telling Kvetzenski that he was assuming command, he went straight to the Vladimir Regiment and ordered it to march around the eastern end of Kourganie Hill and attack the British on their left flank. He placed himself at one side of the column and rode along with it. Kvetzenski later claimed that he did the same, and it may well be that he was the instigator of the move. The explanation probably is that one of the generals set the regiment moving and that the other, riding along on the opposite side when it was already under way, subsequently came to believe that the movement was his own idea.

In any case, whoever set it in motion, this massed column of 3,000 Russian infantrymen, with a front of eight files, came tramping resolutely around a corner of Kourganie Hill, making straight for the Great Redoubt. The front files advanced with fixed bayonets, their muskets held at the ready preparatory to a charge. There was nothing hurried about the column's advance; it had little appearance of a charge, but that was its intention—to cut down the mass of British soldiers in the Redoubt. The column was intended to act as a plowshare, the front files and ranks along each side forming its cutting edges. If one of the edges was damaged by casualties, then the next files and the next ranks remained to slice their way through. But the column never cut into the mass of Codrington's men, because by the time it reached the Redoubt the British had gone.

There was no immediate panic when the column was sighted. Had it not been for a chain of untoward events, the British might well have driven the Russians back. But as soon as the column came into sight and individual British soldiers started to shoot at it, someone shouted, "Don't fire! They're French!"

There was, in fact, no similarity between the gray coats of the Russians and the blue uniforms of the French. But everybody knew that the French were somewhere in the vicinity, and in the tension of battle the cry was enough to implant doubt and to cause a check; the firing stopped. Then a bugler

in the British lines sounded "cease fire," as if officially to confirm the order. He afterward asserted that an officer whom he
could not identify had come up and ordered him to do so, but
his vague description was never pressed to an inquiry, because
it probably would have been impossible to get to the truth
when the units were so mixed up. Surprised at the check in
firing, the Russian column halted. This served to confirm the
doubt that had been implanted about its nationality, so other
buglers took up the "cease fire." Then, just as inexplicably,
someone sounded the "retire."

In judging these events, it has to be remembered that the
troops in the Redoubt had no military formation at all, and
consequently no acknowledged chain of command. Men were
torn between their instinct to await orders and their realization that no orders were likely to be forthcoming. The buglers,
who were the accepted means of disseminating orders—but
who in ordinary circumstances never had to think for themselves—played the unenviable role of sounding the confusion.

With the "retire" call, a state of even greater confusion
arose. Nobody obeyed immediately, but everybody started
discussing whether or not he should.

The officers of the Royal Welsh Fusiliers had managed to
gather together at one corner of the Redoubt, and in an endeavor to set their men an example of solidarity they climbed
to the top of the parapet, there to discuss whether or not the
call should be disregarded. Many men had climbed up the
parapet coming into and going from the Redoubt, but so far
none had lingered on the top. The stationary little group made
an easy target for some Russian sharpshooter, and one by one
the officers of the Royal Welsh Fusiliers were all shot down.

Another bugler repeated the call. A sergeant of the Welsh
Fusiliers, now left in sole command of his battalion, called to

the men nearest him to do their duty and obey the order. And so, because the orderliness on which their discipline was based had been abandoned, the survivors of Codrington's brigade were soon scrambling over the parapet out of the Redoubt and hurrying down the slope toward the river, under a hail of enemy fire.

11

THROUGH THE RIVER IN STEP

Hᴵˢᴛᴏʀʏ ʜᴀˢ ɴᴇᴠᴇʀ ʙᴇᴇɴ too complimentary to Lord Raglan, nor for that matter to any other of the British generals, about the part they played in the Crimean War. According to all accounts, they gave only the most superficial forethought to the way they would bring their troops to battle and, except in the elementary sense of ordering one unit to make a move after that made by another, they never attempted to work out any tactical plan that gave consideration to possible countermoves by the enemy.

Although the conduct of war was properly acknowledged as a science, developed by the great generals over the centuries, it was still not recognized as a science whose study was essential for the professional soldier, even one who expected to rise to the top of his profession. Certainly there were men who did study the science of war, but their interest was mainly academic. There was no need for a soldier, no matter how ambitious, to trouble his head about strategy if he happened to have no interest in it.

This was especially true of the men of the nineteenth-century British army, because full-scale war had for so long seemed unlikely. As understood by most officers, professional soldiering had little or no connection with fighting. The man who did rise to high rank certainly might study the intricacies of peacetime army organization: Lord Raglan, for example, had been concerned with administration; but he had never had to resolve a tactical problem in his life. Nor was there a staff college, or any standard of qualification for promotion that indicated that tactical experience was important for military leaders. Fortunately for Britain, she usually found generals with military genius, like Marlborough and Wellington, when she had need for them. Their generalship was inborn, owing nothing to training, although no doubt enhanced by experience. But when Britain sent her army to fight the Russians in the Crimea, her generals had neither genius nor training, and although some were to show qualities of instinctive leadership—Sir Colin Campbell is an example whom we shall shortly see in action—the conduct of the war was in the hands of men who claimed to be professional soldiers but who were in reality amateurs.

Raglan has often been reproached for not exercising more control over the conduct of the Battle of the Alma. We have seen how he made no effort to draw up any tactical plan before the battle, and how even St. Arnaud's plain hint that some plan was needed failed to prompt him to prepare one. But that he said nothing to his subordinate generals does not necessarily imply that he had not formed in his own mind an outline, at least, of how the battle was to be conducted.

In modern times it has become accepted that, subject to the needs of security, the more widely the plan of a battle is known to the men taking part in it, the greater its success is likely to be. But even in this century, and particularly in the First World War, generals have been known to keep their intentions jealously to themselves. One of the difficulties in the Crimea was the dual command of the combined army that was engaging the Russians—a basic handicap to military success from which Britain and France were again to suffer sixty years later. But while neither St. Arnaud nor Raglan was in a position to impose his ideas on the other, and no concerted plan been adopted which the separate armies were to follow, there is no doubt from the way Raglan held back the British army when the allies first approached the river that he had a clear conception in his own mind of the over-all tactics by which the battle was to be fought, however unimaginative they may now appear to have been.

The part to be played by the British army was surprisingly simple and straightforward: it was to advance directly to the front, assault the enemy positions, and overwhelm them. For this purpose, Raglan had deployed his army in the simplest of all formations—divisions directly behind other divisions, as successive waves of assault. The 2nd and Light Divisions formed the first line of assault; then came the 1st Division; behind this the 3rd and the 4th. Raglan gave the order for the first line to advance. At the same time, he sent an order to the second line—the 1st Division—to "support the Light Division in its forward movement." These were his only orders, but there could have been no doubt in the minds of his divisional generals what their intent was: the first line was expected to attain the objective; the second line was to support it if it needed help; and the third line, although not yet extended, was a last reserve to be brought into action only if the first two lines both failed. This was not a problem of military science; it was simply an exercise of common sense.

Having set this simple, evolutionary tactic in motion,

Raglan considered that he had played his part and that development of the details must lie with the divisional generals; he rode forward to find a vantage point from which he could watch the battle. Only if the whole tactical pattern had to be changed would he be called on to make any further decisions or to give any further commands. He remained in close contact with his divisional generals, still exercising detailed command, while the tactical pattern that the battle was to follow was in the balance; only after he decided to commit his army to a specific course did he withdraw.

Raglan's order to the 1st Division to support the front line went to the divisional general, His Royal Highness the Duke of Cambridge. The Duke was a first cousin of the Queen; their grandfather had been George III. He was only thirty-five, although a balding pate and the assumption of a heavy beard tended to reduce the youthfulness of his appearance. (His beard and the general shape of his features were, in fact, the forerunners of a type that was to grace the throne of England in the later reigns of King Edward VII and King George V.) The Duke had been heir-apparent to the English throne for a short time, because he was born a few months before his cousin Victoria. He was born and brought up in Germany, where his father was a viceroy of the electorate of Hanover before Hanover was separated from Great Britain, and spoke with a German accent. He first took a commission in the Hanoverian army, but when the Hanoverian connection was dissolved he transferred to the British army; with his cousin's help he became the youngest lieutenant general in Britain. He had seen no active service, although, unlike so many other younger officers who were concerned with gaining promotion, he had not needed to spend all his time in England; his connections assured his promotion, so, at his own choice, he served in Ireland, Gibraltar, and the Ionian Islands. His service had instilled in him a sound interest in the affairs of the army. He was a good academic soldier, well versed in the principles of military organization and discipline. He was the only divisional general who had studied the movement and deployment of a division as a unit, and although he came to the Crimea without any knowledge of what war really involved— he was to receive his baptism of fire at the Battle of the Alma— he nevertheless proved his ability as a soldier without any doubt during the Crimean campaign.

Even so, the weight of responsibility for leading directly into battle 5,000 of the nation's most highly regarded troops was considerable for a young general with no active service experience. The 1st Division consisted of two brigades, the Guards Brigade and the Highland Brigade, that were looked on as of quite different quality from the ordinary regiments of the line. The Guards regiments, constituting the Household Troops—the personal bodyguard of the Sovereign—had for long been accepted as forming an elite corps, and the distinction between Guards and Line involved as much snobbery as that between different social classes. In theory, the Highland Brigade was part of the Line, but the regiments that made it up claimed just as distinct qualities as the Guards and were, in fact, regiments to which the people of Scotland looked with conspicuous pride. Perhaps the Highland regiments did not have quite the magnificent appearance of the Guards, whose height and physical stature were accentuated by the towering bearskins on their heads. But while the Guards had acquired their reputation among the people in England for their superb ceremonial performances, and while they had proud battle histories in the Peninsula and earlier campaigns, only a sprinkling of the older men in the ranks of the Guards Brigade that went to the Crimea had seen active service of any sort. No Guards regiment had left England since the return from Waterloo in 1815: it was the accepted duty of the Guards to stay in the country for the protection of the Sovereign, so none of their battalions were sent on routine tours of duty to India or the colonies. In this the Highland regiments had an advantage, and the three regiments from which battalions had been drawn for the Highland Brigade in the Crimea had all seen recent active service.

The Guards Brigade, under Brigadier General Bentinck, was made up of a battalion each of the Grenadiers, the Scots Fusiliers, and the Coldstream. The Highland Brigade, under Brigadier General Sir Colin Campbell, consisted of the Forty-second Regiment (the Royal Highland Regiment, or Black Watch), the Ninety-third (the Queen's Own Cameron Highlanders), and the Seventy-ninth (the Argyll and Sutherland Highlanders).

Sir Colin Campbell was probably the most experienced and able officer in the field that day. He was a contemporary of Lord Raglan and had been commissioned in 1808. He had gone to the Peninsula even before Raglan and had actually fought at Corunna. After the Peninsula campaign he had served in the American War of 1812; he had been to China and the West Indies; but because, unlike Lord Raglan, he had not kept close to the Duke of Wellington nor spent the last forty years in England in the favorable milieu of high society, promotion came to him slowly and laboriously. He had been wounded four times in action, and circumstances had placed him in actual command of a whole division in the Sikh war, but in 1854 he was still a colonel and had only been promoted to brigadier general on sailing for the Crimea. Unlike so many of his colleagues and so many of his seniors, he had learned his profession on active service, in the rugged mountains of Spain and Afghanistan. He had been through every experience that a soldier might encounter, so that he understood his men in a way that was unusual for officers of those days. In modern times, an understanding between officers and men has become part of the science by which good officers are trained, and its development has been accelerated by the social revolution that has removed so many of the old class distinctions. A hundred years ago, the gulf between an officer and a private of the British army was so wide socially that it was virtually impossible for one to understand the other. But Sir Colin Campbell had fought beside his men through situations where artificial distinctions counted for little, and the practical affection that he had always shown his troops was demonstrably returned.

When the 2nd and Light Divisions started to make their arduous way through the vineyards and Raglan instructed the Duke of Cambridge to support the Light Division in this forward movement, the Duke ordered his 1st Division line forward with even more ceremonial deliberation than was affected by the line ahead. Its extreme right, on which were the Grenadiers, just overlapped the road, and its extreme left stretched nearly a mile upriver from the bridge. As soon as the 1st Division moved forward, the 3rd and 4th Divisions, waiting behind in battalion columns, moved outward and took positions to the rear of the flanks of the line—Sir Richard England, with the 3rd Division, on the right; Sir George Cathcart, with part of the 4th Division, on the left. Far away to the left, beyond the 4th Division, the little force of British cavalry under Lord Lucan formed up in column, committed to withstand an onslaught of 3,500 Russian cavalrymen, should these avail themselves of the inviting chance to swing around the British left.

The Duke of Cambridge, for all his ability to handle a division of 5,000 men in line, found himself at a loss when they approached the vineyards and the gardens. If his line moved any farther forward, it would have to be broken up. The front-line divisions were already across the river, trying to sort themselves out on the ledge; Sir George Brown was climbing the bank; General Codrington and Colonel Yea were calling on the first troops to make their assault. Undecided how to move forward, the Duke halted his line short of the vineyards, although General Bentinck, leading the Guards Brigade on the right, was beginning to show some impatience.

General Airey—the Quartermaster General, virtually Raglan's chief of staff—noticed the Duke's hesitation. Airey was always more active than Raglan in urging individual generals to press forward, and when he saw that the 1st Division had halted, while Codrington's brigade was already moving up toward the Great Redoubt, he rode across to General Bentinck. The battalions on the right of the 1st Division, the Grenadiers and the Scots Fusiliers, were suffering heavy casualties, held up as they were in the open on the edge of the vineyards. Bentinck complained to Airey that he understood from the Duke of Cambridge that the 1st Division had been ordered to preserve a wide gap between the two lines. Airey replied that no such stipulation had been made and that the 1st Division should advance closely to support the Light Division's movements; he told Bentinck to convey word to the Duke of Cambridge that the line should keep moving. And so at last the Guards Brigade and the Highland Brigade entered the gardens and vineyards and inevitably came up against the same obstructions that had been met by the regiments preceding them.

The Grenadiers, on the right, staged an almost unbelievable

spectacle. During their whole passage down to the river, and even through the river itself, while the Russian guns kept up a continual harassing fire, they maintained perfect formation for the full length of their line. They moved forward in two ranks, 400 men in each rank; as any section of the line met an obstacle, so was that section hurried around it, and the rest of the line brought up to be formed again. It is doubtful if, as a military movement at the height of a battle, this intricate, laborious process was really necessary. But the battalion had been sent forward in line formation and ordered to cross the river; in the tradition of the Guards, as long as the formation had to be maintained, it would be maintained to perfection. Every few yards, after an obstacle had been negotiated, the line was dressed again and the order given to march forward. The same perfection was maintained when the line came to the river. It marched forward in step, shoulder to shoulder, into the water. Some of the men found the water so shallow they could keep marching; others had to break their step and wade through deeper parts of the stream; some even had to swim; and some, of course, were shot down in the water. But still the battalion moved forward in one line, each man advancing straight ahead, and when it emerged dripping on the other bank the regimental sergeant major called out the company right markers and the whole battalion—or at least those who had survived the enemy fire—stepped forward, took up their dressing, and stood as rigidly to attention as if on ceremonial parade.

The Scots Fusiliers, next in the line, followed suit, but with less precision. Compared with the performance of the Line regiments in the divisions that had gone ahead—few of which kept any real formation—they maintained a high degree of order, but they hardly emulated the superb exhibition given by the Grenadiers. Their colonel was later to write, "The enemy now fired grape at us (very appropriate in a vineyard) which with shot and shell was all about us and plowed up the ground in all directions. How any of us escaped was a miracle."

The Coldstream, on the left of the Guards Brigade, jealous of their own reputation for precise movement, made no attempt to pass through the gardens in line. Their colonel, taking his own initiative, broke the line down into columns of platoons and marched them straight through the vineyards and across the river in that formation. It so happened that ahead of them, as they approached it, the river twists in a sharp S-bend, so that in his determination to adhere to his chosen straight course, the colonel marched his column through the river three times. When he finally reached the farther bank, where Pennefather's brigade had earlier assembled, he extended his platoons and companies back into line and took up formation again with just as much formality and ceremony as the Grenadiers. The entire Guards Brigade had now crossed the Alma River almost as formally as it was wont to march and countermarch when trooping the color before the Queen on the Horse Guards Parade.

12

ROUT OF THE EIGHT BATTALIONS

THE 2ND DIVISION under General de Lacy Evans, on the right of the front British line, which had advanced down to the river astride the road and had passed on each side of burning Bourlouik, had all this time been pinned down on the south riverbank. This was the sector on which Menshikov concentrated the bulk of his artillery; and the constant hail of fire from the heavy guns, particularly those only 200 or 300 yards ahead alongside the Sebastopol road, made it suicidal for anyone to attempt to climb up on to the bank in the manner of Codrington and Yea, who had come to a sector higher up the river to which the artillery had been giving little or no attention.

Then the Russian batteries astride the road were assailed from an unorthodox quarter. The two guns on Raglan's knoll, which stopped firing at the Great Redoubt when Codrington's men swarmed into it, depressed their muzzles and fired down at the Russians from what seemed to the latter to be almost directly overhead. It was a situation with which the Russian gunners could not cope. They turned some of their guns to the west, but they could not get enough elevation to reach Lord Raglan's knoll. Two single pieces were harassing four full batteries, and the batteries could make no reply.

The Russian gunners were so put out by this situation that they started to limber up, and soon all sixteen of the Russian guns that had been commanding the road and the bridge moved back to find less vulnerable emplacements farther up the hill. The guns in the Great Redoubt diverted their attention to Codrington's brigade (and were later silenced altogether), so for the time being the 2nd Division had a respite.

Evans ordered his whole division up onto the bank, and the line was properly extended. But the ground was not as open as that in front of the Light Division. Hillocks rose from each side and walls of ruined buildings stood on the left of the road, so that the only way the 2nd Division could advance would have been to assemble on the road in column. However, Evans did manage to move his troops some way forward, and here they stood firm to check any possible flanking movement by the Russians against the Light Division.

It was half-past three by this time. Colonel Yea and his Fusiliers were still fighting with the Kazan battalion on the right of the Light Division attack, forward and to the left of the 2nd Division's new position. This fight had become quite detached—the turmoil of the rest of the battle went on around it, so that the participants interfered with nobody else and nobody else interfered with them.

Roaring and bellowing, Yea had coerced his officers and noncommissioned officers to sort out his Fusiliers into at least some sort of line formation. Then he wheeled them to face the Russian column, not a hundred yards away. They had hardly achieved perfect dressing, but at least they were in a semblance of a line: there was enacted once again, on a modest scale, the classic contest between line and column.

Wellington had defeated Napoleon on more than one occasion because, against all accepted military theory, he had drawn his troops up in the long thin lines that looked so delicate and vulnerable. Napoleon had pitched his solid columns so fiercely against Wellington's lines that it seemed the lines must break, but again and again each line had stood fast exactly where it was placed and had driven off the column in broken retreat.

The theory to which Wellington had held was simple enough: the longer the line in which are stretched the available men, the greater the firepower that can be brought to bear on the opposing unit. A battalion of a thousand men drawn up in two long ranks presents a front of 500 muskets. A column of the same number of men, assembled in eight ranks, has only a front of 125 muskets when it is drawn up lengthwise to parallel the opposing line; if it is advancing in column it has a front of 8 muskets. In either case, a shattering cone of concentrated fire can be poured onto it from the 500 muskets in line. In those days musket fire was painfully slow, so the number of muskets or rifles that could be brought to bear on an enemy formation was an all-important consideration.

The Royal Fusiliers in line and the Kazan Regiment in column faced each other in parallel formations, closing up until the gap between them was about fifty yards. Only part of Yea's battalion had made its way across the river, so his line was reduced to some 500 men in all, in two ranks of 250 each, covering a front of two hundred yards at the most. It was certainly not a proper battalion line; it had been too hurriedly assembled. But line discipline always determined the behavior of the British soldier, and although the men were not in their

own companies, to be constantly hustled by their own sergeants, they stood up straight, shoulder to shoulder and dressed
by the next man. The Russian column facing this typical
British line was of 1,000 men in eight ranks—125 in each rank
—so its long side stretched about half the length of Yea's line,
and the Fusiliers, although only half the over-all strength of
their opponents, had the immediate advantage of being able to
concentrate twice the firepower.

No British soldier had seen his Russian opponent at such
close range before. The Fusiliers could see the features of the
men they had come 2,000 miles to fight: big, tall men, their
height accentuated by ankle-length overcoats. The Russian
uniforms were all the same, without any distinctive badges of
rank; so, while Colonel Yea conspicuously trailed his sword and
flaunted the trappings of his commission, the Russian commander was hidden in safe anonymity.

For half an hour the two units, the line and the column,
stood and blazed away at each other with musket balls, subject
of course to the limitations of firing frequency that muzzle-
loading imposed. The fight was a musketry duel, each side an
inescapable target for the other, with no cover available and
none sought. The result could only be that the hail of fire
from one side would ultimately wear down the other side.
Although the two never actually became engaged hand to
hand, there was one occasion when a young British officer
ran wildly across to the enemy column, running his sword
through a man in the front rank and hitting out at another
with his fist. For all its heroics this was a dangerous enterprise,
for the officer stood the risk of fire from his own men as well
as from the enemy, and he was in fact killed before he returned to the line. On another occasion a Russian stepped
forward from the column and took careful and obvious aim

at Yea. A Fusilier ran out from the line toward him, to make sure of closing the range sufficiently, and shot him down. The story goes that Yea said, "Thank you, my man. If I live through this, you shall be a sergeant tonight."

When a line stands to engage a column, the commanding officer naturally has to remain either at the rear or on one flank. When Yea saw that his men were composed and holding their own, he sent an officer down to the vineyards on the north bank of the river; he suspected that the reduced strength of his battalion was not due entirely to casualties but that some of his more timid men had held back. The officer did find a dozen or so frightened men—men who must have been genuinely scared if their fear of battle overcame their fear of the wrath of their commanding officer—and, at the height of the Battle of the Alma, while Codrington's brigade was storming the Great Redoubt and the 2nd Division was suffering a devastating barrage of cannon fire, Colonel Lacy Yea had the defaulters brought before him. Having put off their punishment to the next day, he sent them to join the line; no doubt each man hoped, as the musket balls whistled overhead, that death or at least a serious wound would save him from the flogging that was likely to come. Yea knew well enough what little love the men had for his relentless discipline. On the eve of the battle, he had written to his sister, "The Russians are before me and my own men are behind me, so I don't think you'll ever see me again."

Despite the difficulty of distinguishing the Russian officers, there was one man who moved steadily along the ranks, clearly exercising a controlling influence, particularly where the casualties were heaviest and the men tended to get out of formation. After Colonel Yea had dealt with his defaulters and come back to the end of his line to see how the fight was going on,

he ordered that this man be considered an important target.
It is a mark of the inaccuracy and ineffectiveness of the musket
fire of those days that, although the lines were only fifty yards
apart and a line of 250 muskets was pouring out its fire as
rapidly as muzzle-loading would allow, it took some minutes—
and only because a number of men were ordered to concentrate their special attention on the target—before this particular
man was shot down. His removal had the expected effect. The
Russian column lost its principal steadying influence, and
whenever a casualty slumped down to disorder the ranks, the
column seemed to lose its cohesion and even its formation.
Men in the rear ranks, out of sight of the Fusiliers, began to
break away; once started this movement inevitably spread. In
the end the Kazan Regiment, after standing up for more than
half an hour to the Fusiliers—whom they outnumbered by
two to one—simply melted away.

The Fusiliers' casualties were more than 200—almost the
number of one of the battalion's long ranks. But whenever a
man in the front rank had dropped, another had taken his
place from the rear, so that the concentration of firepower
never slackened; although the cost was heavy, the ascendancy
of line over column was once again patently demonstrated.

Once the Duke of Cambridge overcame his hesitation to
send the 1st Division into the vineyards, the Guards Brigade
and the Highland Brigade went forward into the battle without waiting for further orders.

As we have seen, both the Grenadiers on the right of the
Guards Brigade and the Coldstream on the left, after they
emerged from their river crossing, went through the full ceremonial procedure for drawing their battalions up into line. Nor
were the Scots Fusiliers in the center, equally meticulous in

their drill and their bearing, told to rush forward when they reached the top, as Codrington had urged his battalions to do; the battalion had to be halted while the line was formed again. But they rarely went to quite the exaggerated lengths affected by the other two battalions. Whether they lost or gained in military efficiency must be a matter of opinion. Suffice it to say they were the first up the bank and up the slope to the Great Redoubt—an accomplishment which, in the event, turned out to be a disadvantage.

It happened that just at this moment, the first survivors of Codrington's brigade came hurrying back in precipitate retreat down the slope from the Redoubt. Codrington's men, during their first advance, had converged into a mass; retiring, they were still in a mass, a disordered crowd whose prevailing impulse was to escape the shot and shell that were driving them down the slope. This mass bore down on the Scots Fusiliers, whose rigid line could do nothing to withstand it.

The companies on the left of the Fusiliers' line took the main impact of this charge of 2,000 men. The line was completely sundered; men were knocked sprawling, one at least with a number of broken ribs. To add to the melee, the range of Russian cannon fire was progressively lengthening as it followed the retreating men; when it reached the shattered line of the Scots Fusiliers, the whole battalion was forced back in disorder and the men were compelled to jump down again onto the shelter of the river ledge so that they could have a chance to reform.

On the right, the Grenadiers had mounted the bank, and while they were dressing their line again to parade-ground standards they also found themselves in the path of some of the retreating men. But the Guard officers parted the Grenadiers' ranks with ceremonial precision to allow the fugitives to pass through, and although the Grenadiers were also incurring casualties from the Russian cannon fire their line stood fast and immaculate. In a few more minutes the Coldstream, on the left, were up in line too, so that the Guards Brigade now stood at the front of the battle, although there was an unfortunate gap in its center caused by the temporary disaster inflicted on the Scots Fusiliers by their own side.

Sir Colin Campbell soon had his Highland Brigade up on the slope, also. As each battalion climbed the bank and formed line, it immediately moved forward. Quite by chance, the Black Watch on the right was the first battalion up, then the Argyll and Sutherland Highlanders in the center, followed by the Cameron Highlanders on the left; so the brigade line fell into a regular echelon formation, falling back to the left. As the Grenadiers and Coldstream marched forward together, the line of the Black Watch was to the left and slightly to the rear of the Coldstream, and the other two Highland battalions followed similarly, each to the left and rear of the other. So the 1st Division line advanced up the slope towards the Great Redoubt and Kourganie Hill with the Guards Brigade leading in one line on the right—albeit with a wide gap in the center —and the Highland Brigade in echelon to the left rear. It was to turn out to be an effective formation, but one that owed nothing to planning.

When the Cameron Highlanders on the left of the Highland Brigade crossed the river they found General Buller's two battalions, the Connaught Rangers and the Middlesex Regiment—the two leftmost battalions of the Light Brigade— still waiting where they had taken positions before Codrington made his attack: the Middlesex in line, lying down facing the left flank, and the Connaught Rangers in hollow square facing the front. Naturally the arrival of the Camerons on the same ground caused confusion.

Sir Colin Campbell rode over to see what was happening. He did not know that General Buller had remained behind with these battalions, so he sent orders to their two colonels to move forward up the slope. He could not see that they were fulfilling any purpose on the riverbank, and he was an officer who believed every man should be at the forefront of the battle.

Since Buller was waiting with the Connaught Rangers in their hollow square, he naturally learned of Campbell's order when it came to this battalion. Like so many of the other generals, he was an indecisive commander with no experience of battle, but on reflection it seemed to him that Campbell— who was, of course, his equal in rank—was right: now that the supporting line of the 1st Division had come up, the two battalions that were really part of the Light Division line should move forward to their proper place in front. He sent an order to that effect to Colonel Egerton, who commanded the Middlesex Regiment.

Colonel Egerton, however, had his own views. After watching the left of the army for nearly half an hour, he was sure that the Russian cavalry, which could be seen plainly enough massed higher up on the eastern slopes of Kourganie Hill, was bound to move down and attack the flank sooner or later. (This was perhaps a reasonable expectation, and the fact that the Russians never made this move does not necessarily invalidate Egerton's belief that they might do so. Some weeks later, at the Battle of Inkerman, Egerton and the Middlesex Regiment were to exhibit a forcefulness and enterprise that on two occasions virtually saved the day.)

Egerton found himself in a difficult position. His brigadier had ordered him to move, but he was convinced that if he were to comply he would be exposing the flank to serious danger. His hesitation to move to the front of the battle was therefore no confession of timidity; he might well find his battalion in a worse position if he stayed where he was. He sent a reply to Buller, that in the circumstances he did not feel he should be called upon to obey the order. The tone of this message was sufficient to sway Buller from his previous agreement with Sir Colin Campbell's order to move forward, and he reverted to his belief that the duty of the two battalions was to stay where they were.

Sir Colin Campbell was not convinced, but he had no authority over Buller's men, so the Cameron Highlanders marched past the Connaught Rangers' hollow square to the accompaniment of an exchange of uncomplimentary epithets.

When they were clear of Buller's battalions, Campbell ordered the whole of the Highland Brigade line to incline to the left, so that there would be none of the convergence and consequent confusion that had brought disaster to the Light Division.

When the 1st Division line was fully extended, it stretched for nearly a mile and a half, a mighty array of impeccably aligned men, advancing in perfect step, shoulder to shoulder; the front ranks holding their muskets with fixed bayonets aggressively at the ready, the rear ranks with their arms sloped at the precisely correct angle on their shoulders—a spectacle of splendid military exactness. Here was ceremony used in battle, rather than, as was more usual in the British army, formations designed for fighting being used merely in ceremony; the exercise was conducted on a scale, and at a standard of perfection, that had probably never been seen before and was certainly never to be seen again.

The eight battalions forming the column led by General Kiriakov—four of the Minsk Regiments—that by their mere approach (without firing a shot) had driven General Canrobert and his division back down the road toward the river, hesitated to follow him into the ravine. Kiriakov may well have decided that his purpose was limited to keeping the plateau clear of allied troops; and as long as these eight battalions, comprising some 6,000 men, stood at the exit from the ravine, no French force was likely to challenge him. In time, if they could not come out onto the plateau, the French would have to withdraw across the river, again to suffer devastating bombardment by the Russian artillery. Bosquet and his two brigades were clearly content to stay where they were, which was far enough away to be of no real threat to the Russian positions. Of Prince Napoleon and the 3rd Division, still remaining down by the river at the foot of the narrow road, Kiriakov had no immediate knowledge.

But shortly after Canrobert's withdrawal, the guns which he had sent round by Almatamack half an hour before moved onto a road along the crest of the cliffs to approach the head of the ravine. The road ran along a hollow trough, so that neither the plateau nor Canrobert's ravine could be seen from it. The gunners had, of course, no knowledge of Canrobert's withdrawal. The major in command halted his guns and climbed the bank of the road to take his bearings: there, not more than a hundred yards away, stood the eight Russian battalions, virtually in a solid mass. Here was a target of which an artilleryman would hardly dare to dream.

The major unlimbered his guns in the roadway. Although the gunners could not actually see the target, it was easy for an officer to climb up the bank beside the road and direct the fire.

The effect on the Russian battalions was altogether predictable. They had with them no guns of their own to counteract this hidden menace that started pouring round shot and canister into their crowded formation, and it was obviously disastrous for the column to remain where it stood while a succession of cannon balls cut a deadly path through its ranks. Kiriakov had no option but to move the column back toward Telegraph Height.

Despite the pressure that was being put on them by the French guns, the Russians marched away in their ponderous step, in perfect order. As the Russians moved away, the guns followed openly onto the plateau, lining up across the head of the ravine in a position from which they were able to bombard the whole area near the telegraph tower, whither the column had withdrawn. It was the nearest to the center of the Russian positions that any allied guns—except perhaps the pair on Raglan's knoll—had come that afternoon.

The news soon came to the ears of Canrobert's men down in the ravine, and, led by the two Zouave regiments—one of which, it will be remembered, had defected from Prince Napoleon's division—the French soldiers streamed across the plateau with uncharacteristic abandon, not with their ranks actually broken but in amorphous groups with little or no battalion formation, as if, up to now, they had been held back against their will and were straining at the leash to get at the enemy's throat.

At a stage in the battle that was rather later than St. Arnaud had planned, the French army was about to molest the Russian left with some effect. In fact, almost within a matter of minutes, the whole situation on Telegraph Height was completely reversed. So far the Russians had been in full possession of the plateau. Their very presence, and the menace of their guns, had kept the French from venturing out onto open ground—except in the case of Bosquet, who was so far away that he and his men had little influence on the situation. Now the French were to dominate the whole plateau, where it swept westward from the line of the Sebastopol road, while the Russians sought cover from the menace of the French guns.

This startling transformation took place so rapidly that there seems to be no commonly accepted account of how it actually came about. The French were subsequently to claim that they had driven the Russians off in a heroic infantry engagement, but Russian accounts of this part of the battle, which would certainly have tried to emphasize any resistance put up by their soldiers before they were finally compelled to withdraw, make no reference to an engagement with the French. In fact, Kiriakov explains in detail that, when he realized it would be suicidal to remain within close range of Canrobert's guns, he marched the column of eight battalions back toward the telegraph tower. His own batteries on Telegraph Height were still firing down the slope at Prince Napoleon's timid battalions, pinning them down in the vineyards on the north bank and preventing them from crossing the river. This action seemed to require all the Russian guns on the plateau, so Kiriakov had nothing with which to silence Canrobert's batteries. In any case, he was concerned with the safety of the great column of 6,000 men that had been wished on him by Menshikov, and he was still unhorsed; even had he wanted to undertake it, he was unable to set about organizing a redistribution of the Russian artillery to protect his battalions.

After the battle, according to Kiriakov, he first halted his column near the telegraph tower, but when Canrobert's guns came out openly onto the plateau and closed the range, he was forced to withdraw even farther toward the point where the Sebastopol road emerges from the ravine. Here he found more Russian battalions, converging on the road from the other side, whence they were being driven by the advancing British 1st Division line. Kiriakov saw immediately that the only solution was to lead all these units to a new position higher up the road where they could be properly re-formed.

The only Russian infantry formations on the plateau other than Kiriakov's column of eight battalions were four Taroutine and four militia battalions, which, at the commencement of the battle, had withdrawn without orders from the positions in which they had been placed down by the river. A Major Chodasevitch, one of the officers of the Taroutine Regiment, was later to write a faithful account of what he saw of the Battle of the Alma; he too would almost certainly have recorded any engagement with the French at this stage, particularly as there was no other action during the battle with which his own regiment could be credited. But Major Chodasevitch said nothing except that his battalion was forced to withdraw when the French batteries came out onto the plateau. Thus the Russian accounts imply that it was solely the French artillery that drove their infantry away.

The French accounts paint a very different picture of the parts played at this juncture by the men of Canrobert's division and d'Aurelle's brigade. In fact, accepted French history proclaims that the French infantry subjected the Russians to such an overwhelming defeat that the Battle of the Alma was won on the plateau and that the British assaults on the Great Redoubt and Kourganie Hill were minor secondary engagements.

There is no doubt that when Kiriakov moved his column away from Canrobert's guns, the French 1st Division took heart and hurriedly retraced its steps up the ravine to debouch at last onto the plateau. The word soon traveled to d'Aurelle that the French infantry was moving forward, and he too marched his brigade up the road from where it had been waiting and blocking the 3rd Division. Prince Napoleon and the 3rd Division still hesitated.

When these French troops, more than 10,000 in all, emerged onto the plateau and saw the massive Russian column, hounded by Canrobert's guns, marching away in precipitate retreat, their Gallic exuberance was unbounded and they surged forward, as we have seen, with little respect for proper military formation. It had taken time for the 10,000 men to climb the steep roads, so when they came out onto the plateau Kiriakov's retreating column was more than half a mile away. (It was at this moment that the British Guards' Brigade, two miles upstream, was forming line on the south riverbank, preparatory to its advance up the slope to Kourganie Hill.)

The French soldiers were still comparatively fresh because, except for the short morning march, they had virtually been standing or sitting about most of the day, and they pressed forward en masse, the Zouave regiments well in the van. Within a few minutes, their colors were hoisted on the telegraph tower —an unfinished brick pillar round which the builders' scaffolding still stood. Men hurrying forward across an open space will automatically set their course toward a prominent objective, and the loose column formations were soon lost altogether as the soldiers converged on the tower. Since they were uniting only from column formation, the change in their array was not so noticeable as when Codrington's men came together from line at the Great Redoubt, but any resemblance to a proper military formation disappeared.

As the 10,000 men pressed forward toward the telegraph

[163]

tower, those in front started firing their muskets in the general direction of the retreating Russians—although they could hardly pretend that they were taking aim or that their shooting had any real effect. Milling about excitedly, they raised a cloud of dust from the parched earth which rose to mingle with the smoke from their muskets, while all the time Canrobert's guns were adding their own bursts of fire to the confusion; so that anyone viewing what was going on from a distance might well imagine that some lively engagement was in progress. Of course, the British could see nothing of what was happening, because their view was cut off by the intervening heights. The chief witnesses were Bosquet and his men—although they were now more than a mile and a half away—and the sailors on some of the French ships lying off the mouth of the river— who were even farther away, and whose view of Telegraph Height was oblique and very circumscribed. However, these witnesses cannot altogether be blamed if they believed they were watching an epic battle, and it is probable that their evidence is the main basis on which was founded the circumstantial story of this great feat of French arms.

(Some months later, the French *Ministre d'Instruction Publique* sent a certain Baron de Bazoncourt to the Crimea to obtain evidence for writing the story of the part played by the French at the Alma. When he came to this stage of the battle, the Baron gave a circumstantial account of how Kiriakov had rallied the Russian battalions near the telegraph tower and turned them to face the French, supported on right and left by Russian batteries that poured a decimating fire into the French ranks; and how an advance was made towards the Russian positions by the Zouave Regiments and the Chasseurs d'Afrique, who made forward rushes under heavy fire from successive folds in the ground. Finally, a French colonel of

Zouaves had galloped forward in the best Algerian tradition and led the troops to a bloody hand-to-hand engagement with the Russians in which, to paraphrase the record, the dead and dying were heaped together, trampled on, and smothered by the other combatants, while the men who were fortunate enough to escape this unhappy fate lunged at the enemy with their bayonets and drove them from the field.)

Accounts of a heavy engagement tend to be discounted by the known number of French casualties suffered in the whole battle that day: only three officers and fifty other men were killed outright, and the total number wounded did not exceed 500; and there were no other active fights in which French infantrymen were engaged during the battle, either hand to hand or in musketry duels—except in the case of the skirmishers who preceded the columns down to the river. There is no doubt that both Canrobert's and Prince Napoleon's divisions suffered considerable casualties from Russian artillery fire when they were approaching the river crossings. With only half a hundred men killed in all, it must be inferred that most of the casualties were incurred at the river. Even had more men been hit while assaulting the telegraph tower, there could not have been the number claimed by the Baron's report that the Russian guns first decimated the French ranks and that in the ensuing fight the dead and dying lay about in heaps.

However there is, in some accounts, a suggestion that the French soldiers rushed forward so impulsively that they did in fact suffer casualties from Canrobert's guns, which were trying to keep up their harassment of the Russians over an ever-increasing range. Gunnery in those days suffered mainly from inconsistency of charges; it was always risky for gunners to fire over the heads of their own troops, because there was no guarantee that the shots would not fall short. So it is quite possible that some casualties were caused in this way. However, whatever the truth of what happened on the plateau between four o'clock and half-past four that afternoon, the Russian left was broken. But the break came too late for St. Arnaud to be able to claim with justice that the French had turned the flank as the initial tactic from which the course of the battle was to flow.

13

FINALE ON KOURGANIE HILL

I<small>T WAS THE NATURE</small> of the ground, more than anything else, that kept the operations of the French and British armies entirely disconnected. The ravine that carries the Sebastopol road divided the field of battle into two distinct parts—almost into two separate worlds: the high plateau to the west and the hill-studded ground running down to the river to the east. Neither British nor French could see how the battle was faring with the other. Since the armies had no link, even toward the rear, their commanders were equally disconnected. Lord Raglan could see the whole of the British army, but he had no idea of what the French were doing behind him. St. Arnaud, down by the riverbank, was even ignorant of the movements of his own army. It was, in fact, as if two separate battles were being fought, with the trend of one having little relation to the other; and yet the two sectors lay side by side.

At the time when 10,000 French infantrymen and Canrobert's guns were chasing the Russian battalions virtually off the plateau, the British lines only a few hundred yards to the east were still re-forming along the riverbank, facing sixteen

Russian battalions on the slopes of Kourganie Hill. From his knoll Raglan could see, almost directly below, the 2nd Division line, established astride the road but prevented from further advance by the uneven ground and the obstacles before it. Forward and to the left of the 2nd Division, Colonel Yea's battalion was gathering itself together, closing up its ranks. It was badly mauled; as Timothy Gowing wrote, "Our poor old Colonel exclaimed, 'A color gone! And where's my poor old Fusiliers? My God—my God!' And he cried like a child, wringing his hands."

The Kazan column, driven off by the Royal Fusiliers, was also reassembling a quarter of a mile away, on the Russian left of the Great Redoubt. Raglan could see Sir George Brown riding across to speak to Yea. Sir George had spent the whole course of the battle moving about the lower part of the slope, a little bewildered by events which the near-sighted general could not properly see. There was a bright splash of blood on the flank of his horse, flowing from an open wound in the animal's side, but Sir George himself was miraculously unscathed. Yea expressed his determination to take his Fusiliers in pursuit of the Kazan column as soon as they were re-formed, but Sir George told him to move his battalion aside and let the Guards go forward.

In the gap between the two guards battalions where the Scots Fusiliers should have been, Codrington had rallied some 300 men who had been driven back from the Great Redoubt. He managed to form them into a line, two deep. Then, hesitating to place men of the Line alongside the Guards without consent, he asked Colonel Hood of the Grenadiers if these 300 men could fall in on the left.

The Colonel curtly refused. His refusal could be mistaken for arrogance, as if he were carrying the distinction in regimental status to absurd lengths, but in truth it was probably prompted by a hope that the Scots Fusiliers would soon rally and recover their place in the Guards Brigade line; for a little later, after the Grenadiers had advanced some way up the slope, Colonel Hood saw eight isolated men of the Line, survivors of the Sherwood Foresters, still carrying their regimental colors, and spontaneously invited them to take their place on his left. In fact, just as the Grenadiers were moving forward, the first company of the Scots Fusiliers did climb the bank and place themselves in their proper position, so that the gap in the line was partially filled. In immaculate order, the Grenadiers and Coldstream marched forward up the slope, the left side of each battalion dangerously open to any flanking movement the enemy might make.

Taking advantage of the lull that followed Codrington's withdrawal, the Russian columns had disposed themselves in positions that threatened anew the advancing British battalions. In front of the Redoubt stood two battalions of the Vladimir Regiment—part of the column that had been mistaken for a French unit by Codrington's men. These were the leftward battalions of that column, to which Prince Gorchakov had attached himself. It will be remembered that Gorchakov and Kvetzenski had both joined the column unaware that the other was present. The misunderstanding had been corrected, and Kvetzenski now stood with the two rightward battalions in the Redoubt itself. On the Russian left of the Redoubt stood the remains of the two Kazan battalions that Yea's Fusiliers had driven back. To the right rear were two more battalions of the Kazan Regiment, and spread across the extreme right of the Russian line were eight battalions that had come round Kourganie Hill, standing in three columns—one column with four battalions of the Uglitz Regiment and the other two columns

[169]

each consisting of two battalions of the Sousdal Regiment. The Guards' and Highland Brigades, no more than 5,000 men, faced some 15,000 Russians.

When the Guards started to advance, Gorchakov, riding on the left of his two battalions, marched them forward directly down the slope in the Russian version of the infantry charge— at a walk, with bayonets held at the ready by the outer ranks. Their line of charge happened to be directed toward the gap between the Grenadiers and the Coldstream which one company of the Scots Fusiliers could hardly fill. If the three units— the Grenadiers, the Coldstream, and the Vladimir—had kept on their courses, the Russians would have passed between the Guards battalions. But when the distance between the Grenadiers and the Vladimir column had closed to less than a hundred yards, Hood halted the Grenadiers. With the Russians still advancing on their left front, Hood wheeled the left platoon of his battalion with a precise parade-ground movement, so that it hinged back at an angle to the Grenadiers' line and faced directly toward the Russian column.

The front thus presented to the Russians was no more than twenty men, but when the front rank of the platoon was ordered to open fire the immediate effect was to stop the Russians in their tracks. The Russians returned fire as best they could, but they were in an awkward position. The British line that was assailing them was short, but it stood diagonally across one of the corners of their column, so that neither the front nor the side ranks had a proper field of fire. (When men stand in close ranks, the degree by which they can angle their fire is naturally limited by their neighbors' presence.)

While the Grenadiers were able to inflict casualties as fast as they could reload their muskets, their own lines were hardly touched. To add to the Russian discomfiture, the Coldstream, which had halted in line with the Grenadiers, opened fire too. One of the advantages of line formation is that each man in the front rank can cover a wide field of fire from left to right; although the Vladimir column was well to the right, every man in the front rank of the Coldstream was able to fire at it. On the other hand, the oblique line of the Coldstream presented only a narrow target to the Russians. Nevertheless the Vladimir battalions held their ground, although they were suffering heavy casualties, so that their ranks were soon encumbered by dead and groaning men.

Hood had been watching the two Kazan battalions, driven off by Yea, that were regrouping on the Russian left of the Redoubt. Although they were still some way off, they stood on his right front, so that he hesitated to give all his attention to the Vladimir on his left. It soon became evident, however, that after their experience with the Fusiliers these Kazan battalions had no intention of challenging another British line. When he judged that there was no threat from their direction, Hood pivoted the whole line of Grenadiers on the point where the left platoon had previously swung back, bringing forward his right shoulder so that the front of his battalion now had a clearer field of fire at the Vladimir column.

Gorchakov himself faced the British fire bravely, riding up and down in front of the column, exhorting his men to hold their positions and keep up their fire against the British line. In effect, by wheeling the line toward the Russian column, Hood gave the Russians a better target, but at the same time his own men now had a chance to concentrate all their 400 muskets on the much shorter front of the Russian column.

The superiority in firepower soon began to tell. Gorchakov's horse was hit and killed. In fact, it is a miracle that the animal and its rider survived as long as they did. Gorchakov

fell heavily to the ground, striking his head and suffering a con-
cussion. He struggled to his feet, still dazed, and staggered away
from the column. Kvetzenski, who had been sitting his horse
by the parapet of the Redoubt, rode over to speak to him;
Gorchakov gabbled something about all the officers of the
Vladimir Regiment having been killed and then stumbled away
around the end of Kourganie Hill.

The continuous fire by the Grenadiers generated the usual
thick cloud of smoke. The Battle of the Alma was fought on
an almost windless day; the morning breeze had dropped, and
during the afternoon the smoke of battle hung over the field
as if it were loath to disperse. Soon all that the Russians could
see, in the intervals when the smoke from their own muskets
drifted away, were the tall bearskins of the Guards rising out
of the haze.

Inevitably, when Gorchakov left them the Russian battalions started to falter, and soon they were no longer return-
ing the fire with any intensity. Hood gave to his Grenadiers
the command, "The line will advance on the center! The line
will advance firing!" Still as if on the barrack square, despite
the gaps in the ranks where men had fallen and the thick smoke
that made dressing difficult, the battalion wheeled back to its
proper front and moved forward in a well-dressed line, as the
men brought their muskets up to their shoulders, fired, and
reloaded on the march. For a few minutes the Vladimir battalions held fast; then they suddenly broke into retreat, hurrying away in disorder in the direction of the Kazan battalions
on the Russian left of the Redoubt, who joined them and made
for the Sebastopol road. Here, just at this time, Kiriakov was
shepherding the battalions that were retreating from the
French, so for the first time units from the two separate fields
of battle joined in the same, but unhappily rearward, movement.

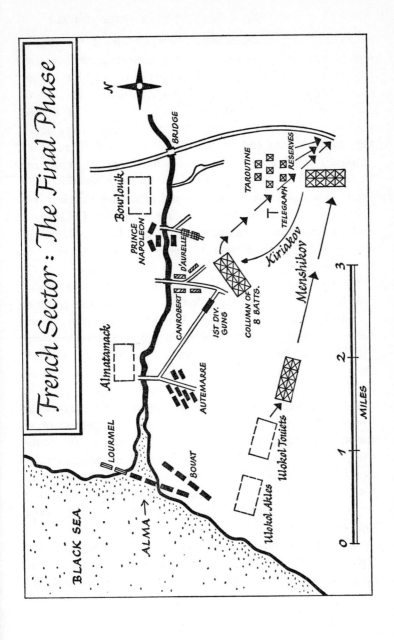

French Sector: The Final Phase

Witness of the dissolution of half the Vladimir Regiment, and threatened by the approaching lines of Grenadiers and Coldstream, General Kvetzinski thought of nothing but hastening to remove the remaining Vladimir battalions. His line of retreat around the west of the hill was already cut off by the proximity of the Grenadiers. Since the battalions were standing at the eastern end of the Redoubt, he led them, at an unusually rapid pace for a Russian unit, straight across the Coldstream front. Almost immediately his horse was shot from under him, and he received a wound in the leg that left him unable to walk. Under the advancing fire of the Coldstream, his men lifted him onto a litter of muskets and carried him after the column (he was soon to receive two more grievous wounds).

But even though the General entertained retreat, the colonel now left in command of the column was not prepared to retire so precipitously from the fight. On the Russian right of the Redoubt stood two battalions of the Kazan Regiment—the battalions that had been driven away by the Green Howards early in the engagement, when Codrington's men first came up from the river. The Vladimir battalions drew up alongside, so that four battalions stood together. By marching across the Coldstream front, the Vladimir had taken themselves out of the line of advance of the Guards' Brigade. It was axiomatic that the Guards would not change their course but would continue marching straight ahead. But the Vladimir and Kazan battalions were now in the direct path of the Black Watch, the rightmost regiment of the Highland Brigade, advancing up the slope only slightly in the rear of the Guards.

The ground on the eastern slopes of Kourganie Hill is steeper than before the Great Redoubt. It is broken by gullies and strewn with rocks, so that, when advancing over it, the

Black Watch line became uneven. Sir Colin Campbell had no intention of allowing one of his battalions to engage the enemy in this state. The whole success of line formation depends on perfection of alignment, so that each man has his full field of fire, without being hindered by his neighbors. The Black Watch were halted and the ranks were dressed—imposing lines of tall men in tartan jackets and trews, their height accentuated by the long plumes that stood up proudly from their Highland bonnets. Then, firing as they advanced, the Highlanders in their turn broke yet another Russian column.

Each of the two other Highland battalions—the Argyll and Sutherland and the Camerons—engaged a Russian column in the same way; in their case, a double-battalion column of the Sousdal Regiment. Twice more, the same story was repeated, although in both instances the Russians put up a stiff resistance before they were finally broken. In all these engagements there was no hand-to-hand fighting; each was a musketry duel, and the side that could not endure the firepower of the other broke and retreated before an actual clash. The results cannot fail to suggest that the qualities of the Russian infantry—their discipline under fire and their bearing in the ranks—fell short of those of their British opponents. But even so, much of the reason for the way each battalion of the 1st Division line broke a column of the enemy, usually twice its strength, without any apparent difficulty, was the superiority of line formation and the shattering firepower that it produced.

There was still a chance that the Russians at the eastern end of the hill might rally. Seventy-five hundred men had been driven in that direction in retreat, but there were another four battalions—3,000 men who had not yet been engaged with the enemy—waiting around the end of the hill. These were the four battalions of the Uglitz Regiment, whose colonel now drew them up so that they blocked the path of the retreating battalions.

Fortunately Lord Lucan, the British cavalry commander on whose meager force Raglan was relying to hold off the massed cavalry of the Russians should they threaten the British left, had decided to bring his squadrons across the river, although he had been given no authority by the commander in chief to do so. (That was in line with Lord Raglan's indulgent methods; he never objected to his generals' initiative so long as their enterprise led to success, for it relieved him of the need to give too much attention to their affairs himself.) Since Menshikov did not seem to be going to use his cavalry—in any case, now the Russian infantry was in retreat it was too late for the cavalry to be of any real danger—Lucan crossed the river at the eastern end of the front, even beyond Buller's still-waiting battalions. The cavalry, accompanied by a battery of horse artillery, climbed the bank that here slopes quite gently up from the river and arrived at the forefront of the battle at a moment so opportune it is a pity to have to admit that it was unplanned.

The colonel of the Uglitz was rallying the retreating Russians, forming them up in a great column with the Uglitz Regiment itself. Even if this column had moved forward, the British would doubtless have prevailed once again, but this was a unit 10,500 strong that would not have broken easily. Yet when the artillery that Lucan brought began firing into its midst, the great column broke before it really had been formed, and the British drove the remains of the Russian army completely from their sector of the field of battle.

When Prince Gorchakov stumbled away from the battle around the western end of Kourganie Hill, he came to the

Sebastopol road and dragged himself up the hill without any real consciousness of what he was doing. It so happened that Prince Menshikov, who was still darting mercurially from one sector of the battle to another without once making an effective decision, was riding down the road. For the first time that afternoon the commander in chief and his second in command faced each other. The battle was in a critical state; plainly there was need for urgent counsel; but the exchange that followed between the two generals was hardly on the executive level. Menshikov demanded, "Why are you on foot? Why are you alone?" and Gorchakov, holding his head, replied, "All my officers have been killed or wounded. I myself have received six shots." Pitifully, he showed the rents in his clothes to his commander in chief, as if they were of far more import than the condition of the Russian army.

Menshikov rode off angrily, and Gorchakov stumbled up the road. Lower on the hill, Menshikov met the retreating battalions of the Vladimir Regiment, and he sought vainly to turn them back to face the enemy. But no spirit to fight was left in the men, and for the first time Menshikov heard murmurs, even shouted cries, of defiance of authority.

In truth the battle was over, and the Russians were being driven decisively from the Alma. The one man who seemed to keep his head was General Kiriakov, who took it on himself to regroup battalions from all the sectors as they converged on the Sebastopol road. The battalions, driven off by either the French or the British, instinctively made their way to the road by which they could most easily withdraw to the safety of Sebastopol. Kiriakov led the column of eight battalions from the French sector up onto a ridge, where for the time being they were shielded from Canrobert's guns. Having established a definite position, he was able to divert to it some of the Russian battalions as they followed each other in precipitate with-drawal from the battle. He was also able to direct thirty guns, which naturally were withdrawing, too, into position along the front of the ridge. So at this late juncture in the battle he man-aged to establish what might have been a formidable defensive position. But this new line was fully two miles from the tele-graph tower, and although it might have discouraged any further advance by the allies it was too far away for even its guns to have any effect on the French, who were massing on Telegraph Height.

Even Prince Napoleon at last ventured with his division onto the plateau. His men were drawn up with Canrobert's troops in some semblance of massed formation on the open plain between the telegraph tower and the Sebastopol road. The excitement in the French ranks was positively tumultuous. A British aide-de-camp who rode over with a message for St. Arnaud from Raglan, and who was more accustomed to the silence scrupulously maintained in the ranks of the British army whatever the circumstances, reported later that in his estima-tion 20,000 French soldiers were all talking at once.

The message that Raglan sent to St. Arnaud was direct and to the point: Was the French army ready to join the British to pursue the retreating Russians? St. Arnaud's reply was equally direct: No further move forward could be made by the French soldiers until they had gone back across the river to pick up their packs.

Like the French, the British were assembling on the ground they had won from the Russians. The lines were redeployed in columns of companies, and the whole British army stood on a wide arc that swept across the lower northern slopes of Kour-ganie Hill. Lord Raglan rode down from the knoll to the divi-sional generals gathered in the center near the Great Redoubt.

As he made his way along the lines, his soldiers naturally cheered him as if he were the fountain of their success.

Raglan was not content to stand upon the victory that had been won. It had always been the Duke of Wellington's rule to pursue a defeated enemy, if he possibly could, and to complete his rout. Without any consideration of the tactical implications involved, Raglan sought to find troops that he could send forward. The 1st, 2nd, and Light Divisions had been fighting heavily, and their men were clearly too exhausted to go any farther. But the 3rd and 4th Divisions and the cavalry, although on the march or in the saddle from early morning and held in readiness throughout the afternoon, had not actually engaged in combat and were still comparatively fresh. In any case, there was only an hour and a half before the sun would start to set, and in that latitude the twilight was comparatively short. So although he had received one refusal from St. Arnaud, Raglan sent his military secretary, Colonel Steele, once more to the French to propose that the British 4th Division and cavalry go forward matched by St. Arnaud with an equal number of French troops.

Raglan would have been willing to send his men forward on their own, but, since the two armies had set forth on this expedition allied in a joint endeavor and had fought side by side to rout the Russians—whatever may in fact have been each army's relative contribution to success—it was essential for the sake of accord between their two countries that they claim an equal share of the credit. (Naturally this hope was rudely shattered as soon as the different accounts of the battle came to the ears of the world.) Raglan had his Government's instruction that his primary consideration at all times be the preservation of allied accord—to this end he had gone out of his way to humor St. Arnaud on frequent occasions—and he feared, with some justification, that if he sent his troops forward on their own to clinch the victory he would be accused of seeking enhanced kudos for Britain at the expense of France.

St. Arnaud was no less adamant than before in refusing Colonel Steele. Again, the need to recover the packs was given as an overwhelming consideration. It might have been that St. Arnaud was impressed by Kiriakov's new line on the horizon to the south. He would certainly have been rash to agree to re-open a full-scale battle; unlike Raglan, he had no cavalry, so the French could not play quite the same part in a pursuit. But the new Russian line looked more formidable than it really was; it was progressively melting away, as one battalion after another disintegrated and groups of soldiers set off on their own to join the stream of men flowing southward in utter disorder along the Sebastopol road.

The slopes of Kourganie Hill were littered with profuse evidence of the dreadful mutilation and physical disfigurement that even nineteenth-century arms could achieve. Perhaps the evidence was grimmer in the days before armies provided attention to the wounded. Corpses may serve to mark the imbecility of war, but they lie quiet and uncomplaining. It is the men who are still alive, repulsive in their wounds and frightening in their agony, who proclaim the inhumanity and horror of battle. In modern war, shattered men are sought out and removed. In the nineteenth century there was no provision in the British army for attending to the wounded—that is to say, before the country learned the lesson of the Crimean War. The bandsmen—a handful of buglers and drummer boys—were used ostensibly as medical orderlies, but they had no medical knowledge, no equipment, and little capacity for sympathy. And when casualties occurred on a large scale, these bandsmen were too overwhelmed for any attempt to go out to deal with them.

The suffering men lay where they had fallen; whether anyone came to their succor depended entirely on the outcome of events. If the allied armies had followed in pursuit of the Russians that evening, the wounded might well have been left behind on the hillside to look after themselves or to die. As it was, individuals in the various regiments sought out their friends, to give them water and try to make them comfortable where they lay. There was nothing that could be done to relieve their pain. But everyone who moved among the wounded in the field that night remarked on their patience and their fortitude; they asked quietly for water and wondered how long it would be before they were moved. A subaltern wrote, "I am willing to believe that our surgeons did their best, but still some poor fellows, unseen or unsought, passed their night in sleepless groans on the field of battle."

Actually, it took two days to shift all those British wounded who could not walk. Each man was picked up awkwardly by two comrades and carried in agony more than four miles to the river mouth, where he was lifted into a boat and taken through the unquiet surf to a ship lying offshore. Painfully, he was hoisted aboard, and, because it was impossible to take him below down the ladders, he was left on deck with no protection from the weather and no guarantee that when the ship rolled he would not roll helplessly with it. His destination was Scutari, on the Asia Minor shore of the Bosporus, where the infamous military hospital had been established in a bare stone Turkish army barracks, and where his chance to survive proved to be almost negligible. Wounded men were sent to Scutari to die rather than to be healed—and to die, in most instances, of diseases contracted in the hospital itself. Several

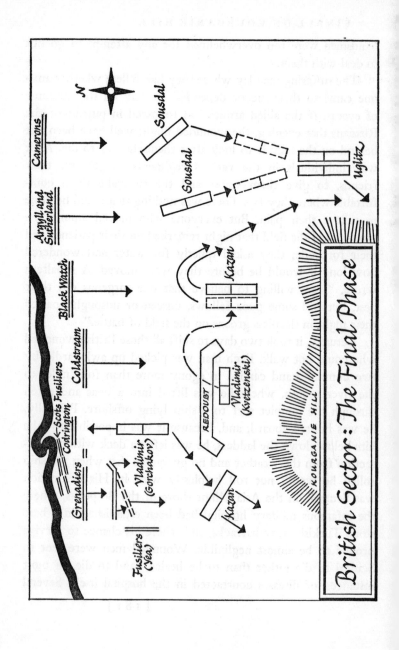

British Sector: The Final Phase

months were still to pass before the miracle that was Florence Nightingale came to the barrack hospital at Scutari, and few of the casualties from the Alma lived long enough to benefit from her ministrations.

The Russians suffered the heaviest casualties in the battle, officially put at the precise figure of 5,709 killed and wounded. There was no number given of those killed outright. The French lost 60 killed, including only three officers, and the number of their wounded has been given as 500, although these numbers were much exaggerated in subsequent reports. The British casualties were officially accounted for as 362 killed, including twenty-five officers, and 1,640 wounded on the field, but these figures take no account of those who succumbed in transit to, and at, Scutari.

It is known that three-quarters of the men in the British army who died in the Crimean War died not at the hands of the Russians, nor even from illnesses contracted on service—and cholera took a considerable toll—but from diseases they caught in the hospital. To be sent to Scutari was virtually a death warrant; ultimately the British victims of the Alma must have amounted to more than a thousand men. Nineteen British soldiers were posted as missing, recorded officially as lost in the ruins of the houses by the river. But the army was busy for three days after the battle, burying the dead and carrying the wounded down to the sea, so it is doubtful if any corpses were covered so completely that all the thousands of men moving about never came across them. There were no high explosives, so material damage could not have been great. A round shot might have broken down a wall, but the houses were small and mostly single-storied, so there could have been no large piles of debris. More—probably most—of the missing were drowned in deep pools of the river, their bodies held on the bottom by the weight of their muskets and packs.

Few prisoners were taken at the Battle of the Alma. The Russians took no allied prisoners, but the British did take a few Russians when some of their battalions disintegrated. Apart from the dead, there were more than a thousand Russians lying wounded on Kourganie Hill, in the vineyards on the south bank, and on the plateau. There was certainly no deliberate inhumanity, but for two days the British were far too occupied with their own wounded to give more than superficial attention to the Russians. What these abandoned men must have suffered is indescribable. The heat of the sun was not extreme, but was painful enough for stricken men tortured by appalling thirst. On the third day, 750 survivors were collected, carried down to the river, and laid out in rows in a shady grove. They were perhaps more comfortable, but they were no less stricken.

Three days after the battle, when the British and French wounded had all been evacuated by the fleets and the allied armies at last moved on toward Sebastopol, the Russian wounded who were still alive would necessarily have been abandoned altogether had not an assistant surgeon of the Essex Regiment volunteered to remain behind with his servant to do what little he could for these pitiful creatures. He could not speak their language, he had only the barest facilities for treating them, and in any case they were far too many for him to be of any effective help. He and his servant spent most of their time removing those who died and digging their graves. It had been arranged that a British ship would come to pick them up and carry them across the Black Sea to the Russian port of Odessa, but there was no mention of when the ship would arrive. When, a week later, H.M.S. *Albion* anchored off the mouth of the river, only 300 of the Russians were still alive.

Whether any of them survived the journey to Odessa, and whether they later recovered, is problematical.

And so, the last survivors departed from the battlefield, leaving only the ghosts and the debris on the hills. Ten days before, nearly 100,000 fighting men had converged on the little valley in a campaign the reasons for which hardly a man among them understood. They had come from far across the world to meet in battle on these remote hills, and then they had left. And the Alma River kept flowing quietly down to the sea, the while it washed from its pools and fords all traces of the alien blood and stains of battle.

14

FRUITLESS VICTORY

THE BATTLE OF THE ALMA was the decisive battle of the Crimean War, not because the allies won it but because they did not lose it. Having won, they never turned the victory to account, and they gained no direct advantage from it in their campaign. (A British admiral, who watched what he could see of the battle from his ship, described it as "a tree in blossom which, suddenly blighted, bears no fruit.") But had the allies lost, the war would have been finished, because they would almost certainly have been driven off the Crimean peninsula.

Even as a viable army, they were in a desperately vulnerable situation; as a defeated force they could not have sustained themselves for any period of time. They had no line of communication with any source of supply, they were reliant for their very existence on contact with fleets at one or other of the river mouths, and had the Russians driven the armies back and contained them on the high steppe between rivers, where they would be cut off from ships and from fresh water, they would have been driven to surrender. Even had they been able to retrace their march and return to the beach near the Old Fort, it is unlikely that they could have been successfully evacuated. The British naval commander in chief, Admiral Dundas, had told his Government at the time it decided to invade the Crimea that he could take the army there but that he certainly could not undertake to bring it back again should it be forced to withdraw.

But it was the Russians who were driven back from the Alma. They were severely routed, with more than 5,000 casualties, but this was a relatively trivial misfortune for an army that could draw on three-quarters of a million men; and although they returned to Sebastopol in a state of frantic disorder, when they reached the town and had time to regain composure they were really in no worse a situation than if they had never come out to challenge the invaders. In effect, they lost nothing by their defeat.

Sebastopol was a comparatively strong fortress, by the standards of those days. The allies themselves acknowledged it as invulnerable to seaward attack. The rugged country to the south and east was difficult ground from which to launch an assault by land, and the wide band of water in the harbor made a formidable obstacle to an attacker from the north. The allies, by defeating the Russians at the Alma, had assured their own immediate salvation, but they had disposed of none of the intrinsic difficulties involved in their landing on the Crimean peninsula. Nevertheless, on the credit side it can be said they gained the moral support of a decisive local victory over an enemy they had come thousands of miles to challenge.

The Battle of the Alma was the only occasion in the war when the whole available strength of all belligerents was put to simultaneous use. There were other battles later in the campaign, but never again were the entire French and British armies deployed for action at the same time. Nor, as it turned out, were the other battles to follow any discernible tactical pattern—although the pattern at the Alma was elementary enough in all conscience. The Battle of Balaklava that followed a month later was merely a series of separate empirical engagements: first, the Russians attacked and drove off some Turkish outposts; next, 400 Russian horsemen attacked the Argyll and Sutherland Highlanders and were driven off themselves; then a column of 2,500 Russian cavalry were put to rout by 800 British cavalry of the Heavy Brigade; and finally, in an engagement that lasted five hours in all, the 700 men of the Light Brigade attacked a line of Russian guns in a charge that has become an immortal story. The only other battle on any sustained scale was the Battle of Inkerman, and this had no tactical pattern at all. The Russians merely poured column after column into the attack and the British met the attack and beat it off by a series of desperate, disconnected engagements over which the high command never pretended to exercise any control. At both Balaklava and Inkerman, only small units of the French army were actively engaged. After Inkerman, the war became merely a concentrated investment of Sebastopol, and although there was plenty of desperate fighting, so that casualties were astronomical by the standards of that time, there was never another set battle. The siege of Sebastopol was in effect a battle in itself, a long-drawn-out battle that took nearly a year, a battle in which the elements joined and none of the combatants was ever able to relax. Sebastopol was responsible for many more casualties than those that were incurred in the three distinct engagements that have gone down in history as the important battles of the Crimean War.

The high command on both sides profited little from the lessons they learned on the Alma, if only because similar circumstances never again arose. Except at Inkerman, and then almost incidentally, on no other occasion did a British line challenge an enemy formation. The ground on which the later battles were fought was not suitable for line formation. That is one of the limitations to the use of the line; it always needs a clear open space with plenty of room for maneuver. (On one occasion at Inkerman, a British battalion advanced in line, and on its right, virtually as part of the same formation, a French battalion advanced in column—an improvisation that was characteristic of that shapeless battle.)

Nor did the Battle of the Alma have any noticeable influence on military thought or development. Its impact was quite overshadowed by the siege of Sebastopol, to which it was merely a prelude, and the shattering episode of Sebastopol was to bring about a complete change in the British army. If the Crimean War had continued in a series of engagements similar to the Alma, that battle and those that followed it would have been studied for their tactical lessons in the conduct of a war of movement. But after the Alma, the war developed immediately into a static siege, and it was on the lessons of the siege that all military thought fastened. It was, too, the special circumstances in which the siege was carried on—in particular, the appalling winter—that served to reveal the weaknesses in organization. And, at Sebastopol, there appeared for the first time a new influence in war—the press correspondent. Howard Russell, of the *Times* of London, was the first to reveal to the public what had been conveniently veiled in previous wars: the criminal ineptitude of the commissariat and supply organizations, and the appalling suffering caused by lack of medical services.

At the Alma, the British soldier took these shortcomings as normal. Weather conditions were good and the lack of equipment and supplies—such as greatcoats and tents, forage for horses, and so on—caused no immediate inconvenience. The dreadful plight of the wounded and sick had been accepted as traditional and unavoidable. But when winter came to the Khersonese Upland, from which the allied armies overlooked Sebastopol, no preparations of any sort were made, so that privations became cruelties and the lack of medical attention was sheer inhumanity. Those were the evils which Howard Russell reported to England, and which Florence Nightingale fought, virtually singlehanded, in the wards of the barrack hospital at Scutari. Their efforts bore early fruit, and even before the war was over—that is to say, before Sebastopol had been reduced—the supply and medical services of the British army had been transformed at least into the beginnings of proper organizations. Certainly it took many years for them to develop any degree of real proficiency from this hasty start, but it was the lessons of the Crimean War that set the process of reorganization in motion, because of the thousands of lives that had been sacrificed in striving for such a limited objective.

The Battle of the Alma was a curtain raiser preceding the drama of the siege of Sebastopol. The drama taught its audience a somber lesson, but the curtain raiser was remembered only for the applause it occasioned.

The colonel of the Scots Fusiliers wrote to his mother after the Battle of the Alma, "I cannot describe to you how strong the enemy's position was. The Russian generals we have taken prisoner say they expected to keep us at bay for three weeks. In three hours the enemy were in full retreat. So confident of victory were they that ladies came to see the fight. A bonnet has been picked up, a feather of which I have kept to adorn your own bonnet."

In fact, the allies won mainly because the Russians allowed it. At two stages during the afternoon, the Russians could have delivered devastating blows to turn the battle decisively in their favor. The first was when the British 1st Division was crossing the river and the Light Division was being driven back from the Great Redoubt. At that moment, Menshikov should have sent his ample force of cavalry to strike the British army on the left flank. Part of the cavalry could have struck downriver along the south bank; the rest could have crossed the river and swung in behind the Highland Brigade and the Guards, who were in a highly vulnerable position, drawing up their lines on the narrow ledge between the water and the vertical bank.

The Duke of Wellington proved forever that, in the right circumstances, lines are always superior to columns; but, even so, lines are of little value to infantry being assailed by cavalry charges, particularly if the cavalry attack on the flank and the lines have no room in which to wheel and face the attackers. The accepted infantry defense against cavalry was for each battalion to form itself into a square. Buller had enough room to put the Connaught Rangers in a hollow square at the left of the line, because at that point the bank sloped gradually up from the river; along the rest of the bank there was no room at all. But Buller himself had no illusions about the vulnerability of his position; he knew that a Russian cavalry charge launched at this stage could have thrown the whole British army into chaos. This is not to suggest that the British would necessarily have been overwhelmed; they would doubtless have fought stoutly and might well have driven off the cavalry in time. But the pattern of their attack on the Russian positions would have been entirely broken up, and the formidable Russian infantry battalions on Kourganie Hill could then have moved down to add to the confusion into which the British would have been thrown.

The second occasion when the Russians might have turned the tide was when Canrobert refused battle with Kiriakov's column and withdrew in almost indecent haste down the ravine onto the river ledge. Kiriakov's column was a formidable force and the road down the ravine was ample for its passage, as was shown by Canrobert himself when he took his division up it. If Kiriakov had followed resolutely on Canrobert's heels, there would have been no artillery to embarrass him, and he might well have driven the French 1st Division back across the river. Then, by swinging round to the east, he could have closed the rear of Prince Napoleon's division, which was already in a disorganized, dispirited state.

A bold move like this could have created the same chaos among the French that a Russian cavalry attack could have caused among the British. In neither case is it stretching the imagination too far to believe that the move was possible or that, with a little more enterprise, the Russian commander might have put it into effect. If both moves had been made when the individual opportunities presented themselves, they would have occurred almost simultaneously, and the result would have been devastating to the allies. In any case, it was pure chance that brought Canrobert's guns along the road at the top of the cliff at the particular moment when Kiriakov's column halted at the mouth of the ravine. The passage of the guns was merely one of dozens of movements made during the course of the battle, and had it not been for the chance that brought the gunners to a situation where they were able so easily to inflict damage on the column, it is unlikely that the French would ever have taken the initiative of a direct assault on the enemy.

But the Russian command lacked cohesion; there was no chain of command at all. Menshikov was much too volatile a personality to be entrusted with so many large units, whose greatest need was co-ordination and direction in relation to each other. Lord Raglan at least took a wide view of the battle and saw the part that his army was to play. Menshikov never saw all three sectors at once; while he was moving in one place he was never aware of new pressure exerted in another. He dealt with each incident in the battle pragmatically, and while he was concerning himself with one tactical problem he gave no thought to any others. Moreover, he never considered the problems of even one sector as a whole, but he repeatedly busied himself with some local detail and allowed himself to be carried far away from the central direction of the battle.

Of his three subordinates, Gorchakov was the weakest link. Kvetzenski, until he was put out of action, handled his columns well; Kiriakov showed enterprise and courage. In fact, the whole blame for Russian failure must fall on the commander in chief himself, for he had well-drilled and well-disciplined troops who outnumbered the enemy and held a readily defensible position; at his right hand, waiting simply to be used, was the cavalry which could have given him easy victory. One can only conclude that Menshikov overlooked this possibility simply because he had allowed himself to be overwhelmed by harassing detail in every part of the field. Prepared to place no reliance on his sector commanders, he busied himself first at one end of the position and then at the other. Consequently, at no time had he any true comprehension of the state of the battle as a whole, and he probably never realized when the opportunity to use the cavalry arrived.

Thus Menshikov's shortcomings, rather than Raglan's own conduct of the battle, brought success to the British commander in chief. Although perhaps it is difficult to accept his tactics as good generalship, there is nothing to criticize in what Raglan did, nor, as it turned out, in what he omitted to do, when it comes to the battle. But it is permissible to reflect that had any

[193]

complication arisen to disturb the even sequence of the simple tactics he had adopted, he might not have found the situation so straightforward and easy to handle. The fault was not in Raglan himself; it was in the prevailing indifference in British army circles to the technicalities of war. If, when Raglan was sitting his horse on the knoll, watching the 1st Division making its splendidly ordered crossing of the river, he had seen the host of Russian cavalry sweep down on the British flank from the east, there would have been little that he could have done. The system of communications was primitive. It would have taken twenty minutes for an aide-de-camp to ride down from the knoll and canter along the riverbank with an order to General Buller on the left. And Raglan had no idea at all of what was happening to the French, so if Kiriakov's column had driven Canrobert back across the river, Raglan might well have found his own headquarters cut off by the Russians without any warning.

St. Arnaud was, frankly, no general at all. Admittedly he was a mortally sick man, but all accounts suggest that he was well composed on the day of the battle, and when he had visited Raglan the night before he had shown every appearance of good spirits. But his mind was extremely shallow, and he had no capacity for appreciating either a moral or material situation. He had none of the qualities needed for a general on whose decisions depend the actions and fate of 30,000 men. He tried, before the battle, to inject some tactics into its conduct, but his proposals were jejune; and as soon as his army started to move into position for the battle, he buried himself in the midst of one of the divisions, so that he was virtually out of contact with what was going on during the whole of the afternoon. His greatest tactical error, for which he and his army were fortunate not to suffer retribution, was to dissipate his entire force, so that when the French were most heavily committed they had not the backing of a single man held in reserve.

The British divisional generals were steady, brave men, even though they may not have been blessed with a great deal of technical competence. They were arrogant in manner and outlook but they were enterprising, and in a crisis each one would have used his initiative boldly and aggressively. The behavior during the battle of the French divisional generals, in fact, bears out the estimates of their characters that their histories suggest.

Of the regimental officers, the least prominent were the Russians, mainly because their ranks were submerged, by intent, in the gray amalgam of the regimental columns. The Russian regimental officer was not much less of an automaton than the men he commanded. Everything that was required of him —his behavior, his method of command—was laid down by an authority that ultimately stemmed from the Tsar himself. Although, because of the accident of his birth, he was classed in one of the higher of the fourteen social ranks to which every Russian was assigned, he was given no rein to use his initiative or his individuality, even as an officer.

On the allied side, the French regimental officers were more technically efficient than the British. Most had seen active service in Algeria, and they handled and moved their formations in a businesslike way, well adapted to active service, while the British officers acted as if they were still on the parade ground. Still, there could be no doubt of the courage and purposefulness of the British officers, once disencumbered of social distractions.

It was the British private soldier who was the hero of the Battle of the Alma. Perhaps the French or even the Russian soldier, in the same circumstances and given the same background, would have behaved just as heroically. The Russians had to endure the agony of their columns, and yet, driven perhaps by the duress of suppressive discipline, they stood time and again under devastating punishment before they yielded. Most of the French soldiers had plenty of experience of the privations and dangers of active service, but they were conscripts who accepted only what hardships they had to accept, without looking for more. But the British soldier, although he too was rigidly disciplined and subjected to many social indignities, was a volunteer, and this made just that difference in his reaction to the demands made of him in battle. His realization—if only subconscious—that he was where he was by his own choice, led him to accept the calls made on him in a mood of resigned fortitude. He was drilled to a degree of perfection that made his movements and his bearing almost automatic, but there was something more than mere automation waiting under the surface to respond when the demand was made.

When the Guards and the Highland Brigade marched up the slopes of Kourganie Hill, in lines, in step, in perfect dressing, they were carrying out a movement in which they had been rehearsed to such a degree that its execution was virtually second nature. But they had never been trained to keep on marching while musket balls and round shot sprayed their ranks and the blood ran into their eyes and down their arms and legs, or when it was impossible to dress by the next man because he had just been killed. Nor were they rehearsed in the protracted process of firing, reloading their muskets, ramming home the charge, and firing again, while they stood in line as inviting targets to an enemy not fifty yards away. And least of all were they trained to lie flat on the ground, waiting patiently to be mutilated by a cannon ball, or march through a river, to be shot down, lie disabled in the water, and left to drown.

All this and more the British private soldiers were called

upon to do. Because they endured what they did, and because they carried, up the slopes of Kourganie Hill, the fighting traditions of their fathers and their grandfathers, they won a battle which the men who led them might otherwise have lost.

Before the Battle of the Alma, it was understood between Raglan and St. Arnaud that when the allies reached Sebastopol they would assault it from the north, across the harbor, although no detailed plan had yet been considered. Immediately after the battle, St. Arnaud declared that the only way in which Sebastopol could be successfully assaulted was to march around and approach it from the south. It was a decision to which Raglan was compelled to defer because he found it impossible to gainsay the ailing French marshal; when he came away from his last meeting with St. Arnaud to discuss the matter, he said to General Airey, "Did you observe him? He is dying."

The armies moved from the Alma on September 23, three days after the battle. Because the French had to attend to only a few wounded, they were ready to move two days earlier. Held back by the British, who were engaged with the Russian wounded as well as their own, St. Arnaud became impatient and reported to the Emperor in a dispatch, "What slowness! War can hardly be carried on in this way!"

On September 25, they crossed the Belbek—the last river before Sebastopol harbor—and swung inland to pass around the harbor's head. After a march that took two days, they came at last to the Khersonese Upland, looking down over Sebastopol from the south. Here the British and French armies, and the men who poured in by the tens of thousands because of the appalling casualties, spent nearly a whole year, including a terrible winter, before they finally gained the object for which they had come to the Crimea. Over 300,000 men were killed, wounded, or died of disease in the Crimean War; all sacrificed to take one town.

On the day after the armies left the Alma, St. Arnaud's chronic illness, undiagnosed as were so many mortal sicknesses in those days, struck him down with a virulence he had not experienced before. For months he had suffered recurrent attacks of searing internal pain and now he was to undergo the final agonies until at last he lapsed into merciful unconsciousness. He died three days later. His body was placed in Prince Gorchakov's carriage, that had been captured at the Alma, and carried to the mouth of the Belbek River, there to be placed on board a French man-o'-war.

During the days while St. Arnaud was dying, Raglan, in his unassuming way, virtually took over the combined command of the armies as they marched round Sebastopol harbor— although the French would have been reluctant to admit it. Once St. Arnaud was dead, Canrobert assumed command of the French army by virtue of his commission from the Emperor. He held the command until May in the following year, when, broken in spirit as much by the continuous pressure piled on him to comply with Louis Napoleon's irrational whims as by the dreadful frustrations of the siege, he handed over at his own desire to General Pélissier.

A month later, in June, Lord Raglan fell ill. It has been said he was a victim of cholera, although other reports deny this emphatically. As with St. Arnaud, his illness was never properly diagnosed, but clearly he was attacked internally by some virus that, left untreated, weakened him beyond recovery. He was an elderly man with little physical reserve, nor did there remain within him the spirit to live.

For all his aloofness, he was deeply sensitive to the tribulations of his officers and men. He suffered acute personal distress over the tragedies that beset them through the agony of the winter and the purgatory of the siege. The British Government, the press, and the people heaped virulent criticism upon him, making him their scapegoat for the neglect and indifference to military needs of which they themselves had been guilty for so long. All this had a crushing effect on his body and his spirit, and on June 28, 1855, he died.

The victory on the Alma was his first and last success.

THE BATTLE OF
THE ALMA
September 20, 1854

ORDER OF BATTLE

THE RUSSIAN ARMY

Commander in chief: General Prince Alexander Sergeievich Menshikov

Commander of central sector (also second in command): General Prince Mikhail Dmitrievich Gorchakov

Commander of eastern sector (Russian right): General Kvetzenski

Commander of western sector (Russian left): General Kiriakov

Central sector:

4 battalions	Volhynia Regiment	
3 ”	Minsk Regiment	10,000 infantry
4 ”	Borodino Regiment	
1 ”	riflemen	

4 batteries field artillery (32 guns)

Eastern sector:

4 battalions	Kazan Regiment	
4 ”	Vladimir Regiment	
4 ”	Sousdal Regiment	13,000 infantry
4 ”	Uglitz Regiment	
2 ”	sailors	

Brigade of Hussars
2 regiments Cossacks of the Don $\bigg\}$ 3,400 cavalry

5 batteries of field artillery (40 guns)
14 heavy guns

Western sector:

> 4 battalions Moscow Regiment
> 4   "   Taroutine Regiment ⎬ 10,000 infantry
> 4   "   reserves
> 3½ batteries field artillery (28 guns)

Detached at Ulukol Akles: 1 battalion Minsk Regiment
½ battery field guns (4 guns)

THE FRENCH ARMY

Commander in chief: Marshal Armand Jacques Leroy de St.
    Arnaud

1st Division: General François Certain Canrobert ⎫
2nd Division: General Pierre François Joseph Bos- ⎪
    quet   ⎬ 30,000
3rd Division: General Prince Jerome Charles Napo- ⎪ infantry
    leon   ⎪
4th Division: General Élie Frédéric Forey   ⎭

8½ batteries field artillery (68 guns)
accompanied by 9,000 Turks

THE BRITISH ARMY (Comprising one battalion of each regi-
    ment named)

Commander in chief: Field Marshal Lord Raglan (the Hon.
    Fitzroy James Henry Somerset)

Front line:

> 2nd Division (Lieutenant General Sir George de Lacy
>   Evans)
>> Right brigade: (Brigadier General Adams) ⎫
>>   Welsh Regiment (Forty-first) ⎪
>>   Royal Berkshire Regiment (Forty-ninth) ⎪
>>   North Lancashire Regiment (Forty-seventh) ⎪
>>   (Loyal North Lancs)   ⎬ 5,000
>> Left brigade: (Brigadier General Pennefather) ⎪ infantry
>>   East Lancashire Regiment (Thirtieth) ⎪
>>   Border Regiment (Fifty-fifth) ⎪
>>   Nottingham and Derby Regiment (Ninety- ⎪
>>   fifth) (Sherwood Foresters)   ⎭

Light Division (Lieutenant General Sir George Brown)

Right brigade: (Brigadier General Codrington)
    City of London Regiment (Seventh) (Royal Fusiliers)
    West Riding Regiment (Thirty-third) (Duke of Wellington's)
    Royal Welsh Fusiliers (Twenty-third)

Left brigade: (Brigadier General Buller)
    Yorkshire Regiment (Nineteenth) (Green Howards)
    Connaught Rangers (Eighty-eighth)
    Middlesex Regiment (Seventy-seventh)

} 5,000 infantry

Second line:

1st Division (Lieutenant General His Royal Highness the Duke of Cambridge)

Right brigade: (Brigadier General Bentinck)
    Grenadier Guards
    Scots Fusiliers } the Brigade of Guards
    Coldstream Guards

Left brigade: (Brigadier General Sir Colin Campbell)
    Royal Highland Regiment (Forty-second) (The Black Watch)
    Argyll and Sutherland Highlanders (Ninety-third) } the Highland Brigade
    Queen's Own Cameron Highlanders (Seventy-ninth)

} 5,000 infantry

In reserve:

3rd Division (Major General Sir Richard England) the First, Twenty-eighth, Thirty-eighth, Forty-fourth, Fiftieth, and Sixty-eighth Regiments } 5,000 infantry

4th Division (Major General Sir George Cathcart) the Twentieth, Twenty-first, Forty-sixth, Fifty-seventh, and Sixty-third Regiments } 5,000 infantry

Cavalry: (Major General Lord Lucan and Brigadier General
    Lord Cardigan)

Fourth and Thirteenth Light Dragoons; Eighth, ⎫ 1,000
    Eleventh, and Seventeenth Hussars   ⎪ cavalry-

Artillery: ⎬ men and
  8 batteries field artillery (64 guns)   ⎪ artillery-
  1 troop horse artillery (4 guns)   ⎭ men

Rifle Brigade: 2 battalions

BIBLIOGRAPHY

Airlie, Mabell, Countess of, *With the Guards We Shall Go: A Guardsman's Letters in the Crimea*. London: Hodder & Stoughton, 1933.

Barnes, Major R. Money, *A History of the Regiments and Uniforms of the British Army*. London: Seeley Service & Company, Ltd., 1954.

Fenwick, Kenneth, ed., *Voice from the Ranks: A Personal Narrative of the Crimean Campaign*. London: Folio Society, 1954.

Hamley, General Sir Edward, K.C.B., *The War in the Crimea*. London: Seely & Company, 1891.

Kelly, Mrs. Tom, *From the Fleet in the Fifties*. London: Hurst & Blackett, Ltd., 1902.

Kinglake, A. W., *The Invasion of the Crimea*, Vols. I–VIII. Edinburgh: William Blackwood, 1863–1887.

Rambaud, Alfred, *History of Russia*, Vol. III. Boston: Dana Estes & Company, 1882.

Ross of Bladensburg, Lieutenant Colonel, *A History of the Coldstream Guards*. London: A. D. Innes & Company, 1896.

Slade, Rear Admiral Sir Adolphus, K.C.B., *Turkey and the Crimean War*. London: Smith, Elder & Company, 1867.

Stephenson, Sir Frederick Charles Arthur, G.C.B., *At Home and on the Battlefield: Letters from the Crimea, China, and Egypt*, coll. and arr. by Mrs. Frank Pownall. London: John Murray, 1915.

Vetch, Colonel R. H., C.B., *Life, Letters, and Diaries of Lieutenant General Sir Gerald Graham, V.C., G.C.B.* Edinburgh: William Blackwood, 1901.

Wheater, W., *Historical Record of the Seventh, or Royal Regiment of Fusiliers*. Leeds: printed for private circulation, 1875.

Wood, General Sir Evelyn, V.C., G.C.B., G.C.M.G., *The Crimea in 1854 and 1894*. London: Chapman & Hall, 1896.

Woodham-Smith, Cecil, *The Reason Why*. London: Constable & Company, 1953.

INDEX